EASY PIANO

SONDHEIM SONGS

ISBN 978-1-4234-7273-5

7777 W. BLUEMOUND RD. P.O. BOX 13819 MILWAUKEE, WI 53213

Visit Hal Leonard Online at
www.halleonard.com

ANYONE CAN WHISTLE

from ANYONE CAN WHISTLE

Words and Music by
STEPHEN SONDHEIM

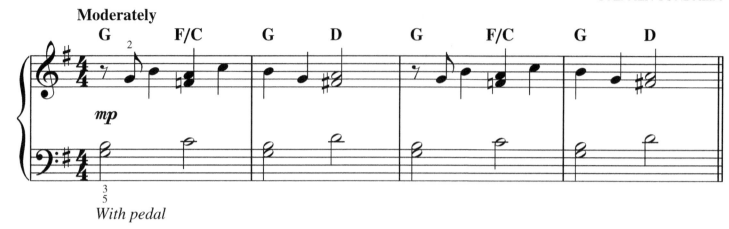

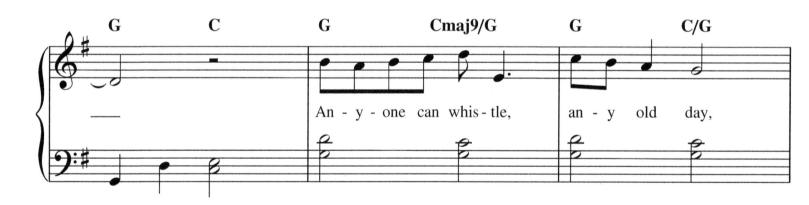

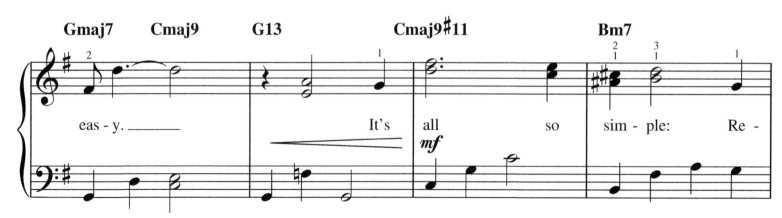

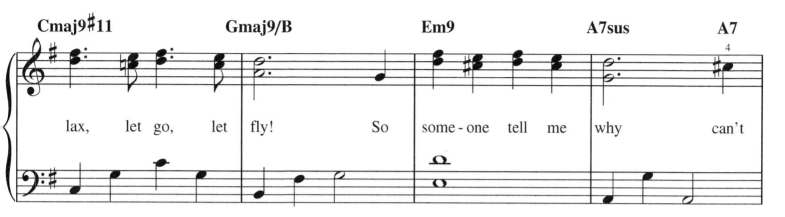

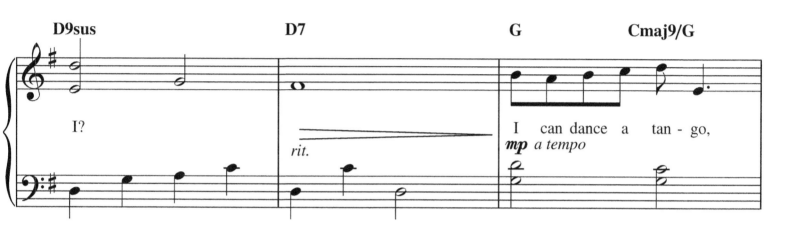

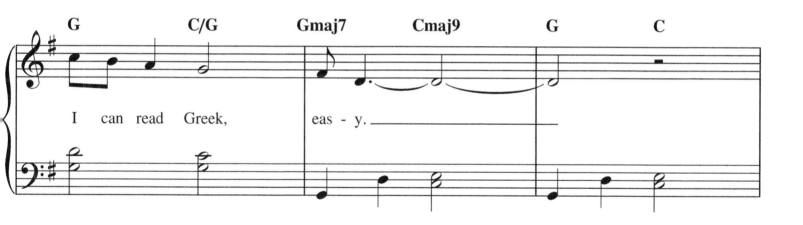

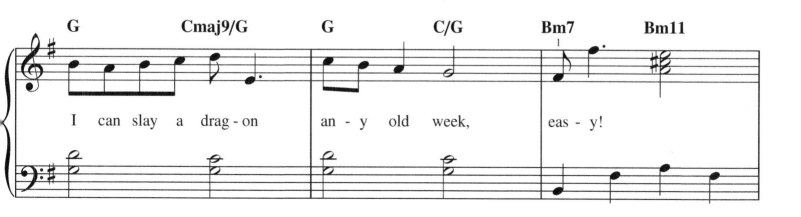

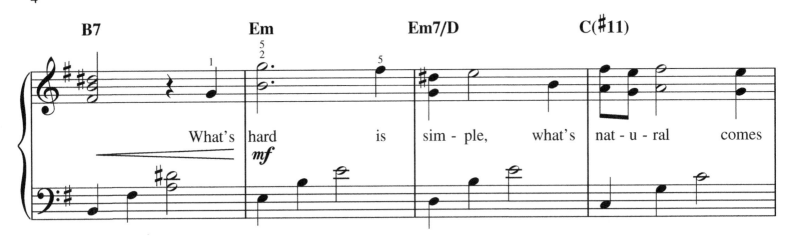

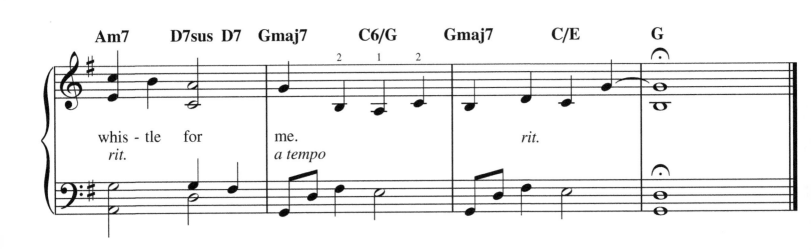

BROADWAY BABY

from FOLLIES

Music and Lyrics by
STEPHEN SONDHEIM

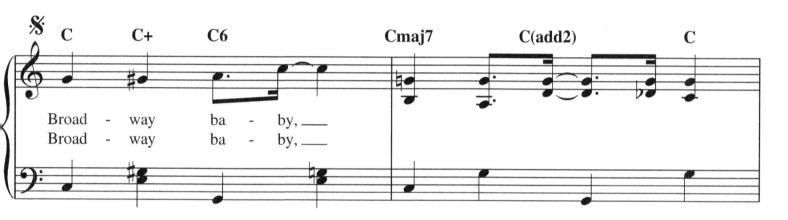

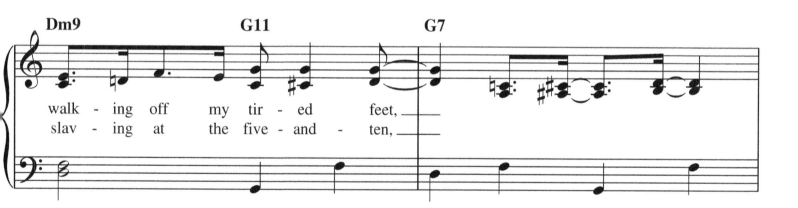

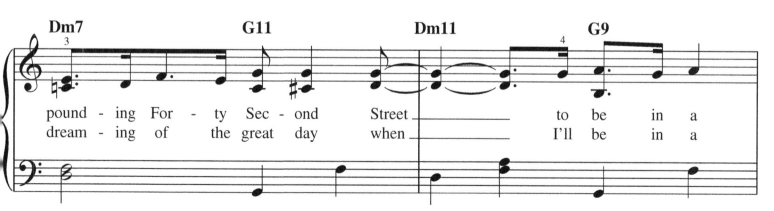

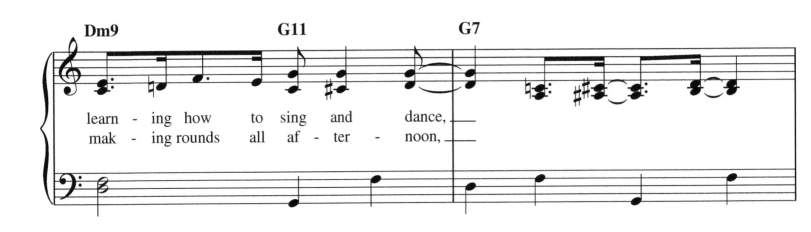

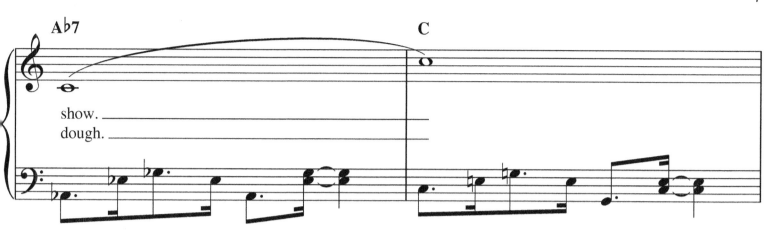

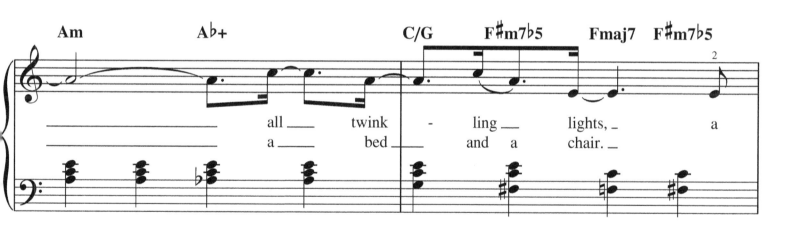

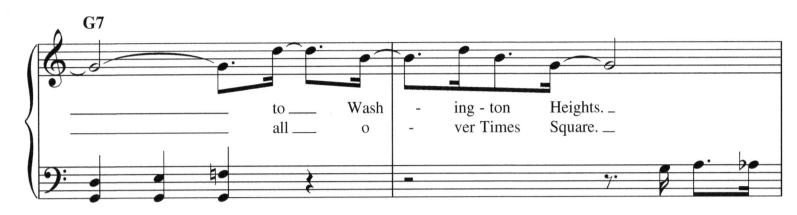

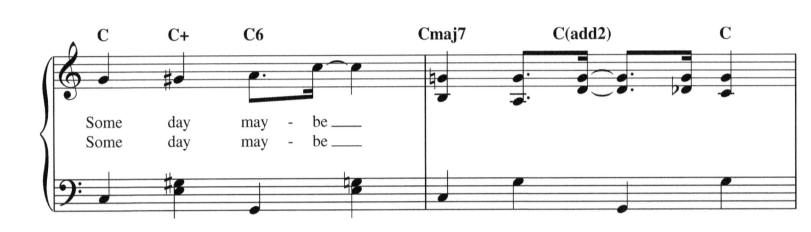

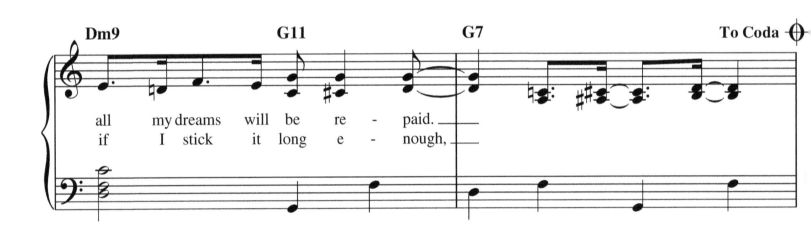

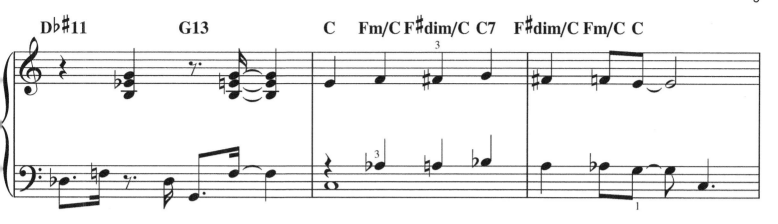

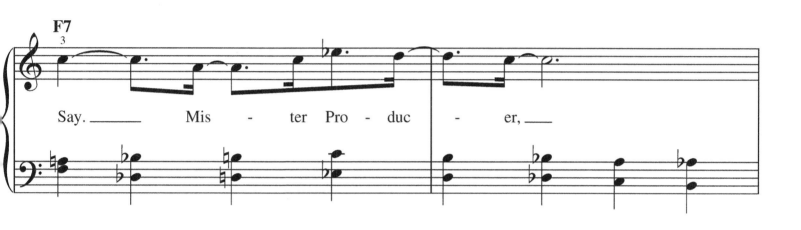

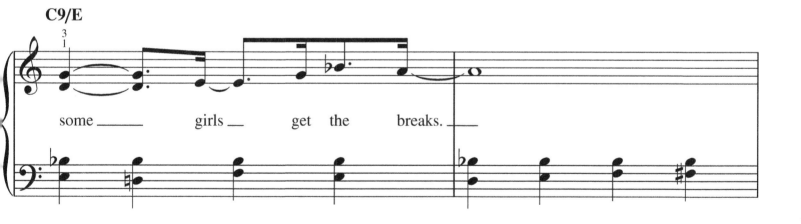

I've _____ got ___ what it takes.

Say, _____ Mis - ter Pro - duc - er, ___

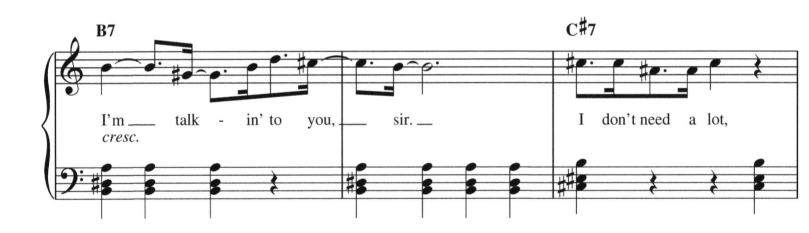

I'm ___ talk - in' to you, ___ sir. ___ I don't need a lot,

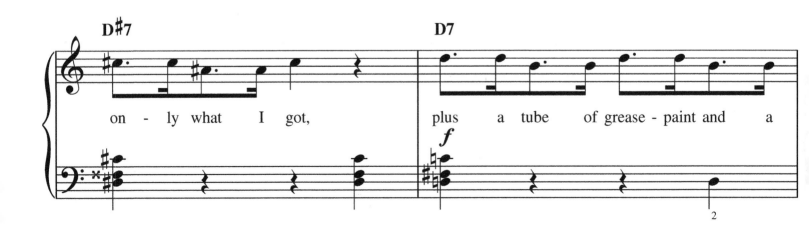

on - ly what I got, plus a tube of grease - paint and a

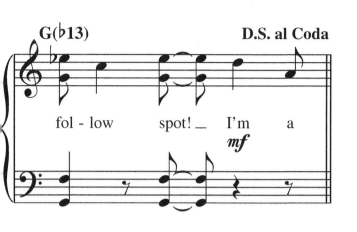

fol - low spot! _ I'm a

I can get to strut my _ stuff, _

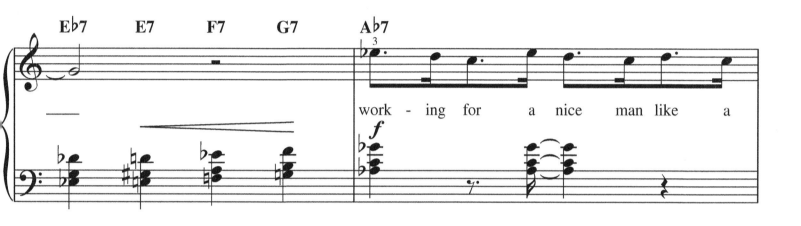

_ work - ing for a nice man like a

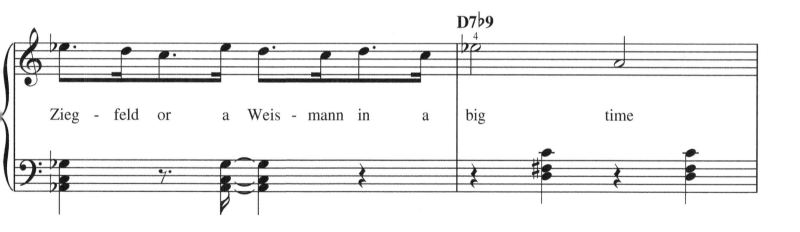

Zieg - feld or a Weis - mann in a big time

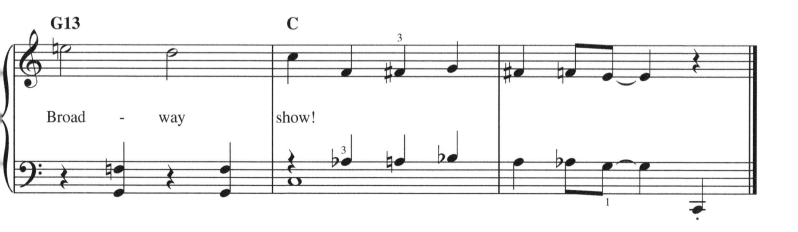

Broad - way show!

CHILDREN WILL LISTEN

from INTO THE WOODS

Words and Music by
STEPHEN SONDHEIM

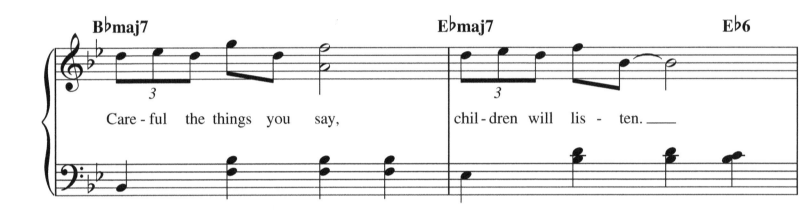

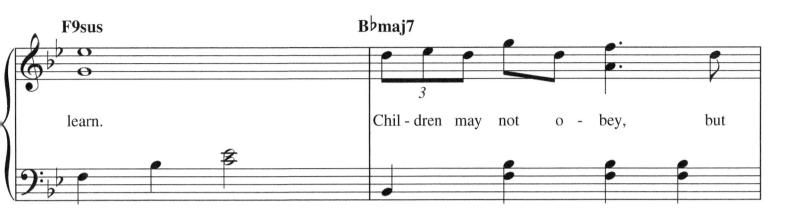

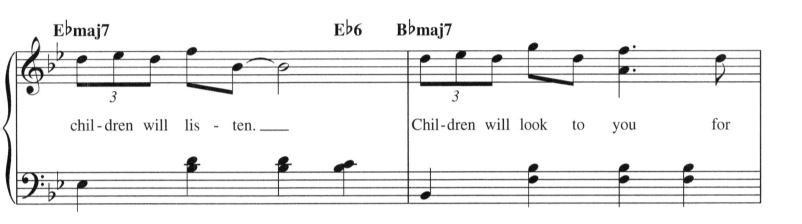

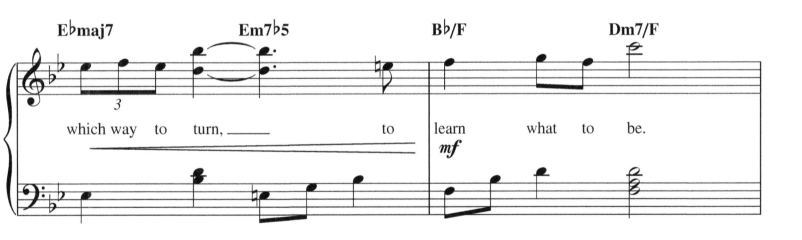

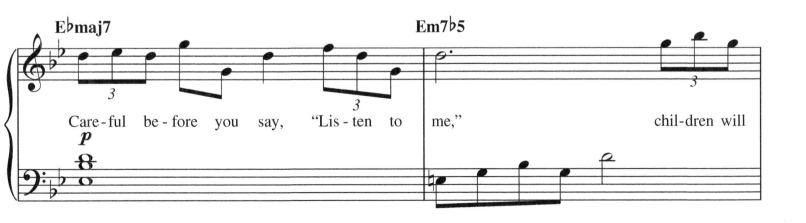

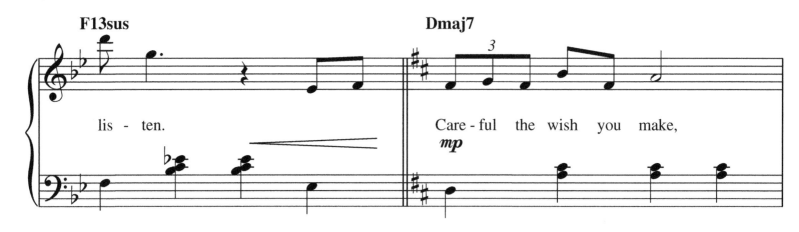

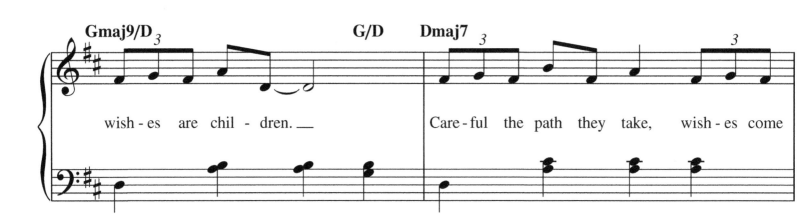

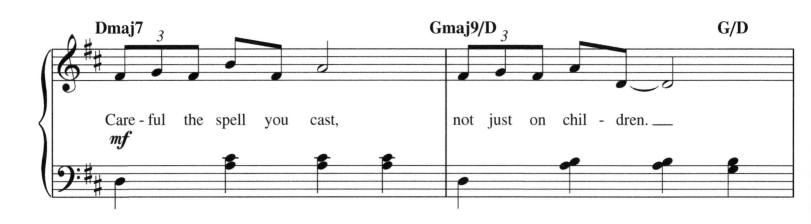

15

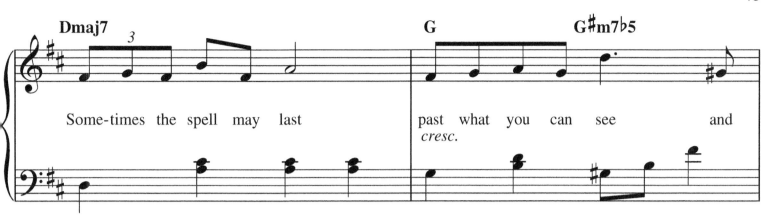

Dmaj7

Some-times the spell may last

G   G#m7b5

past what you can see   and
cresc.

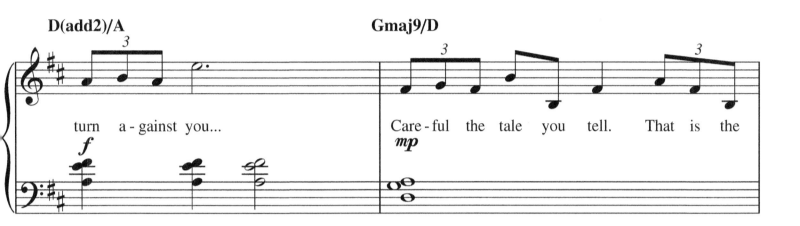

D(add2)/A

turn a-gainst you...
f

Gmaj9/D

Care-ful the tale you tell. That is the
mp

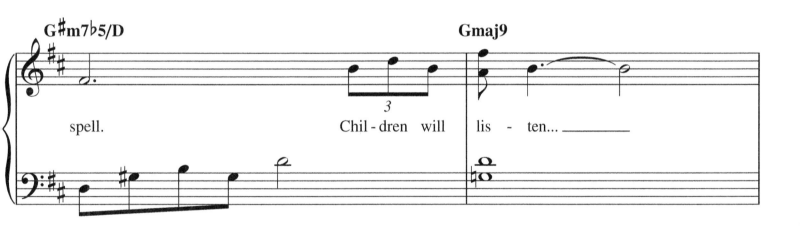

G#m7b5/D

spell.   Chil-dren will lis-ten..._____

Gmaj9

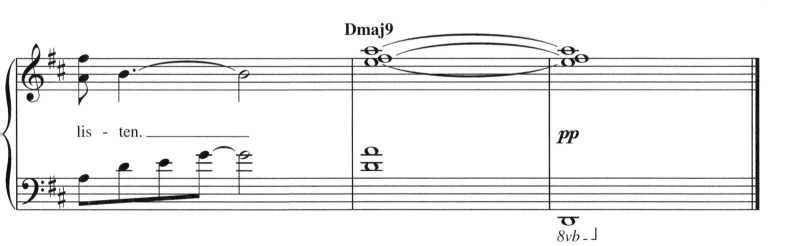

lis-ten._____

Dmaj9

pp

8vb

COMEDY TONIGHT
from A FUNNY THING HAPPENED ON THE WAY TO THE FORUM

Words and Music by
STEPHEN SONDHEIM

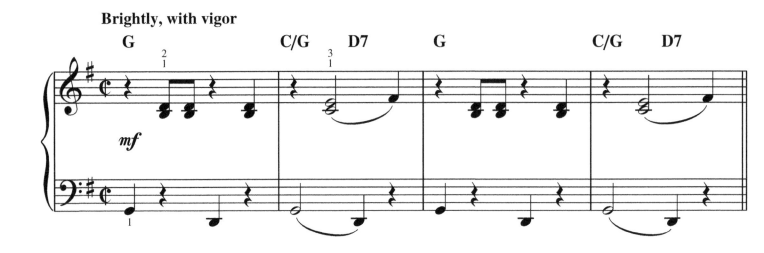

Some - thing fa - mil - iar, some - thing pe -
Some - thing con - vul - sive, some - thing re -

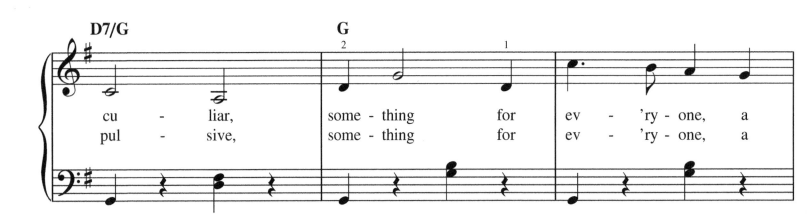

cu - liar, some - thing for ev - 'ry-one, a
pul - sive, some - thing for ev - 'ry-one, a

com - e - dy to - night!
com - e - dy to - night! Some - thing ap -
Some - thing es -

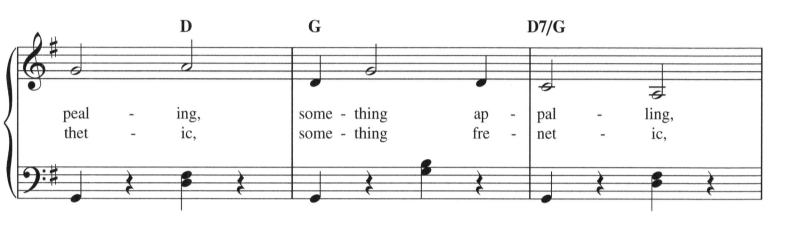

peal - ing, some - thing ap - pal - ling,
thet - ic, some - thing fre - net - ic,

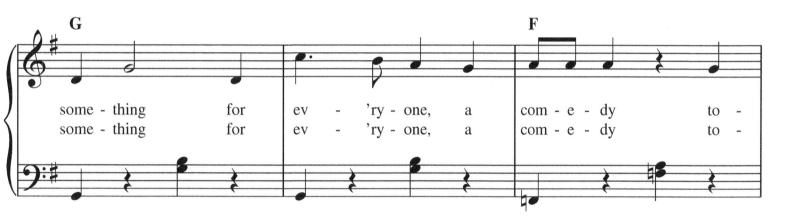

some - thing for ev - 'ry - one, a com - e - dy to -
some - thing for ev - 'ry - one, a com - e - dy to -

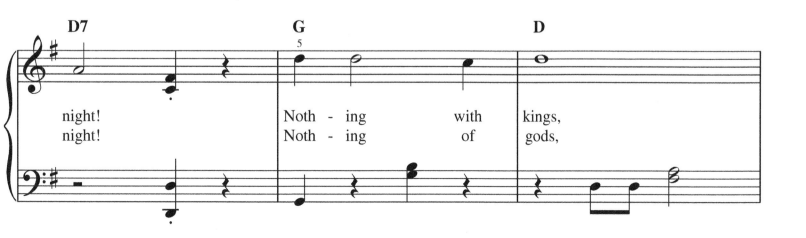

night!
night! Noth - ing with kings,
Noth - ing of gods,

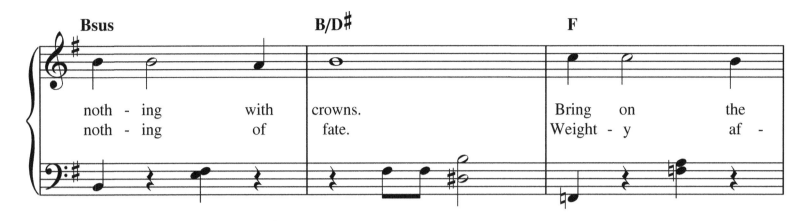

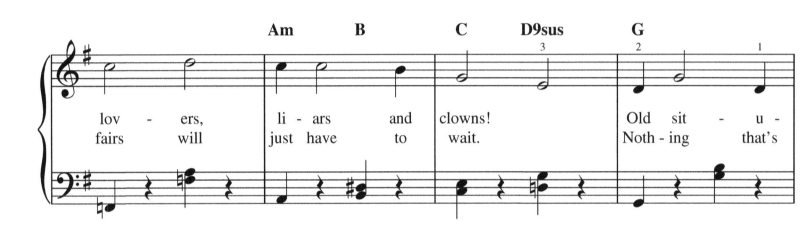

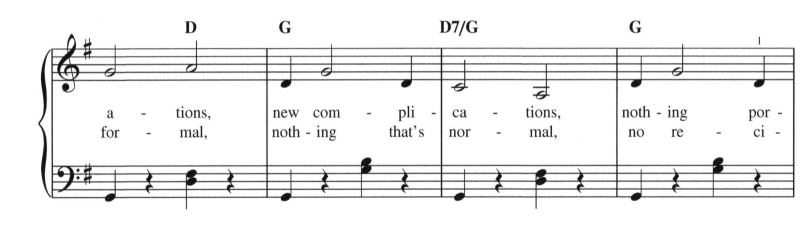

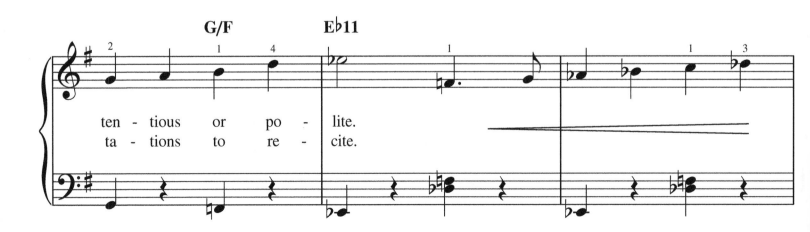

19

GOOD THING GOING
from MERRILY WE ROLL ALONG

Words and Music by
STEPHEN SONDHEIM

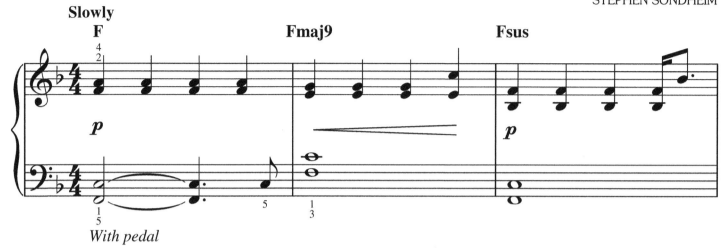

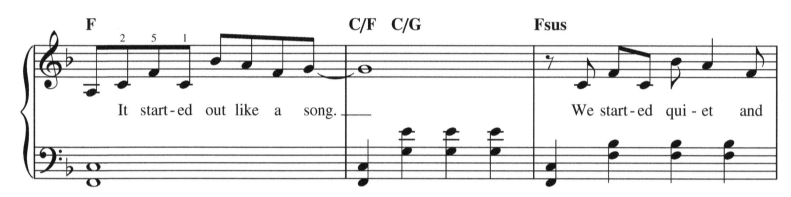

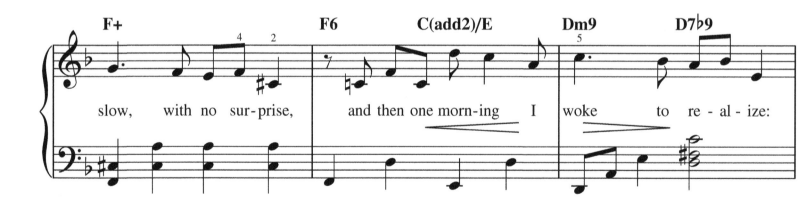

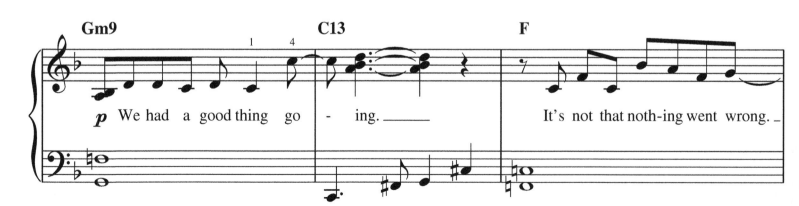

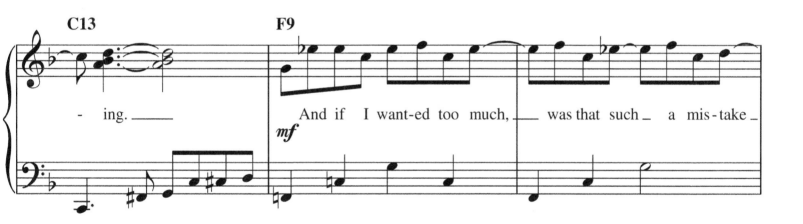

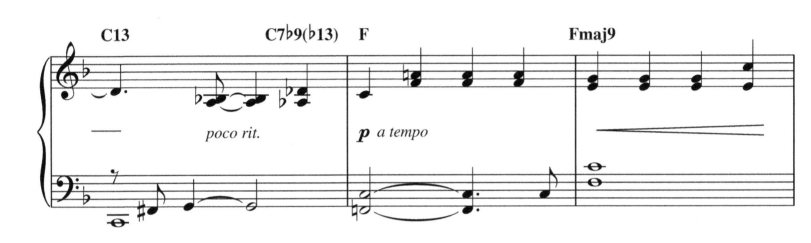

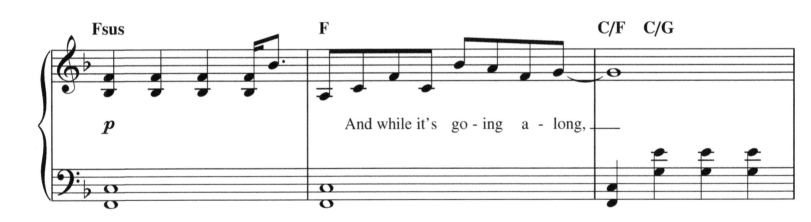

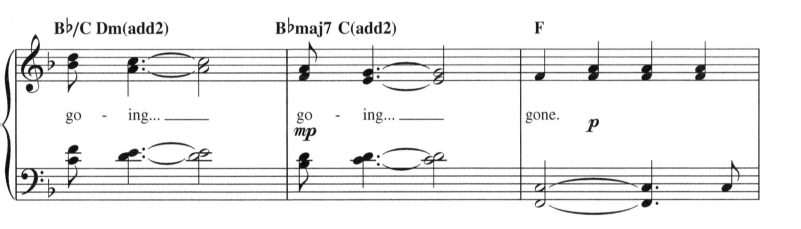

JOHANNA

from SWEENEY TODD

Words and Music by
STEPHEN SONDHEIM

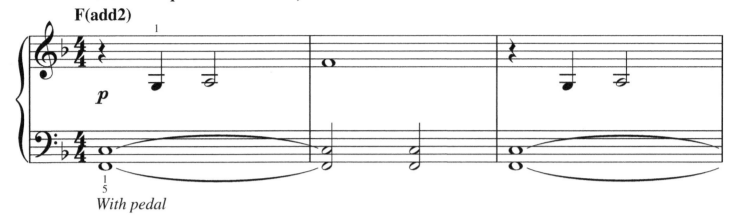

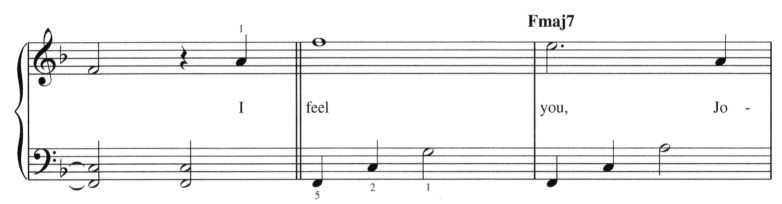

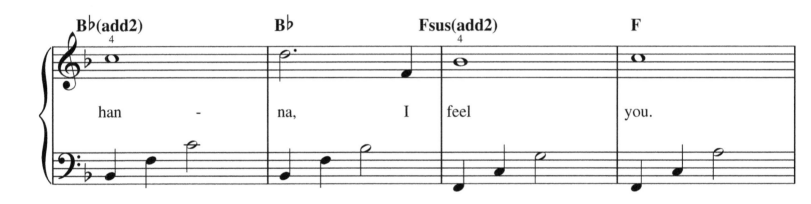

you. Hap - pil - ly, I was mis - tak - en, Jo -

han - na! I'll steal

you, Jo - han - na, I'll steal

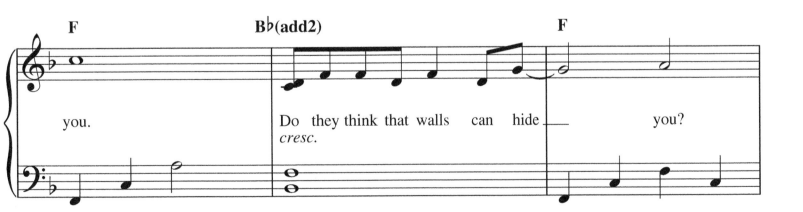

you. Do they think that walls can hide you?

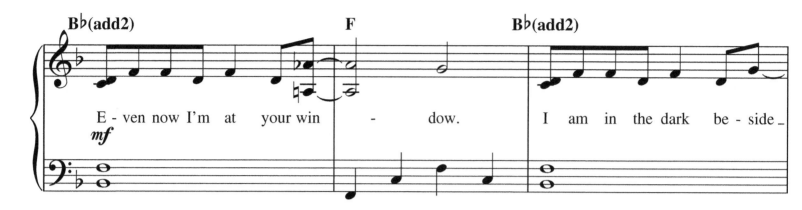

E - ven now I'm at your win - dow. I am in the dark be - side _

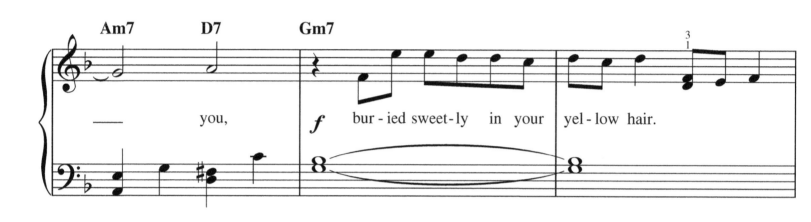

___ you, bur - ied sweet-ly in your yel - low hair.

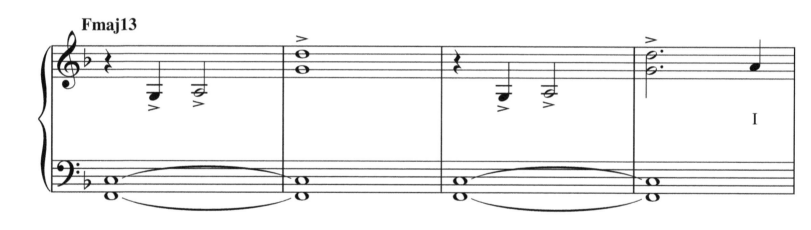

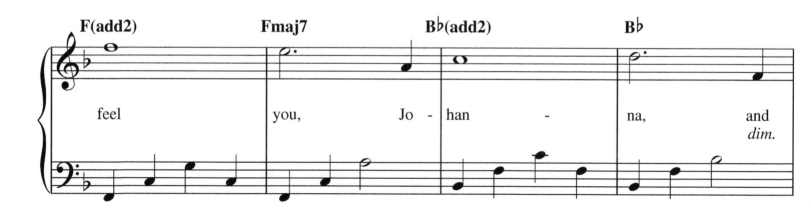

feel you, Jo - han - na, and

LOSING MY MIND

from FOLLIES

Music and Lyrics by
STEPHEN SONDHEIM

Slowly, with rubato

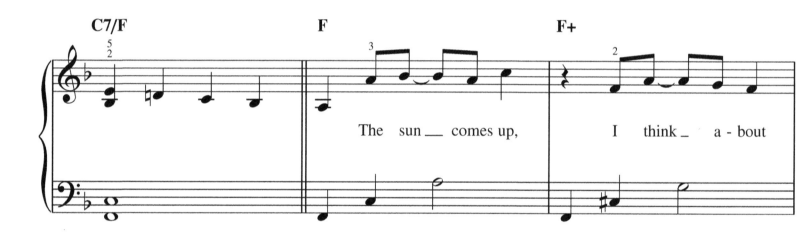

The sun __ comes up, I think __ a - bout

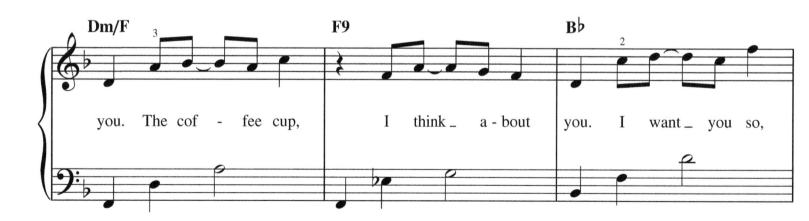

you. The cof - fee cup, I think __ a - bout you. I want __ you so,

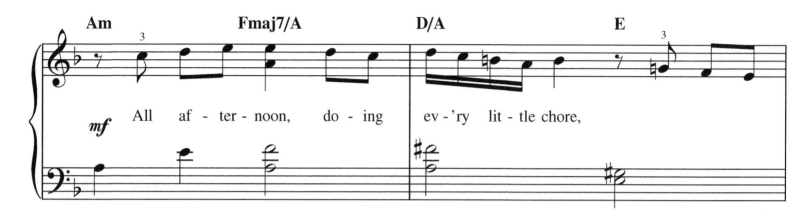

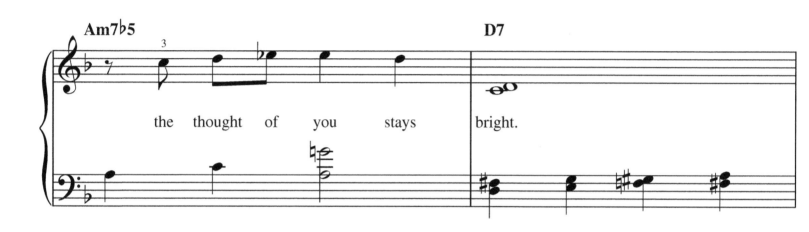

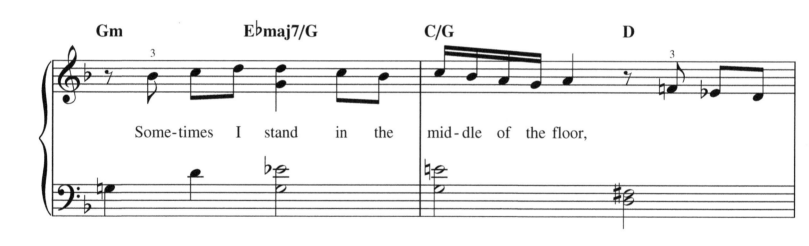

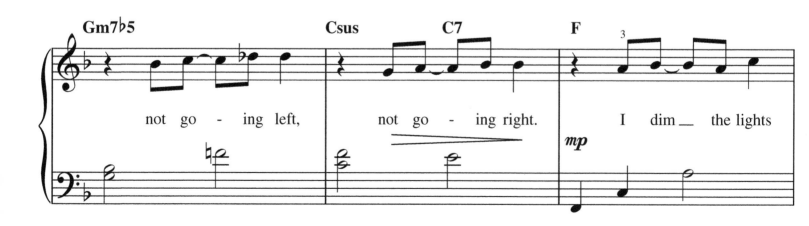

and think＿ a-bout | you, spend sleep - less nights | to think＿ a-bout

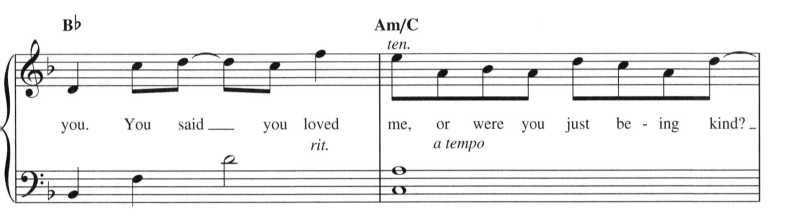

you. You said ＿ you loved | me, or were you just be - ing kind?＿

Or am I los-ing my | mind?

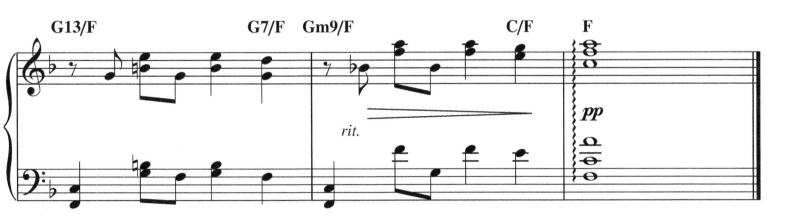

LOVING YOU
from PASSION

Words and Music by
STEPHEN SONDHEIM

Largo tranquillo, in 2

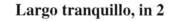

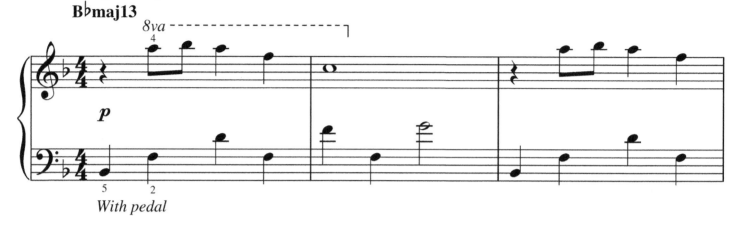

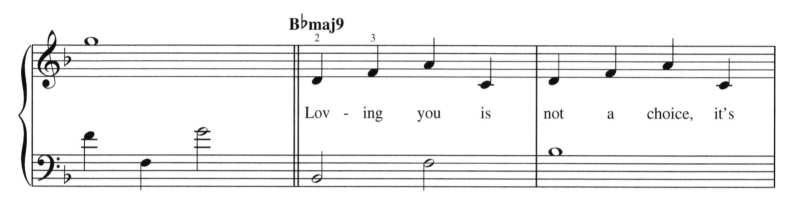

With pedal

Lov - ing you is not a choice, it's

who I am. _____ Lov - ing you is

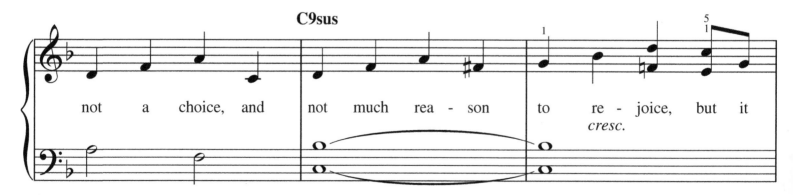

not a choice, and not much rea - son to re - joice, but it

cresc.

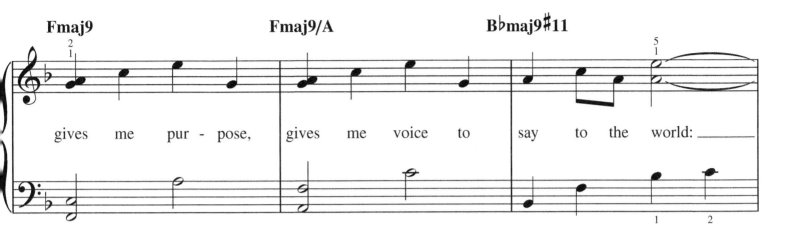

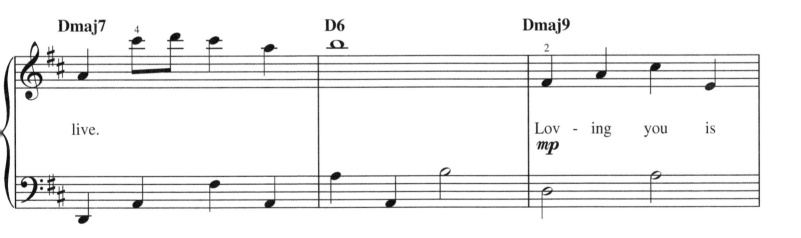

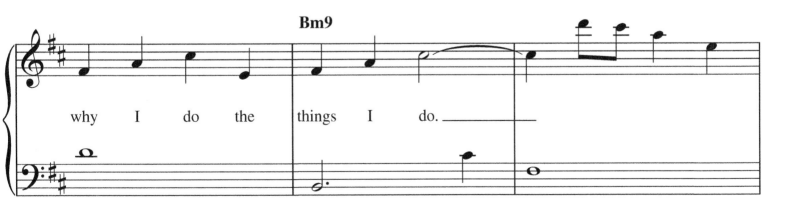

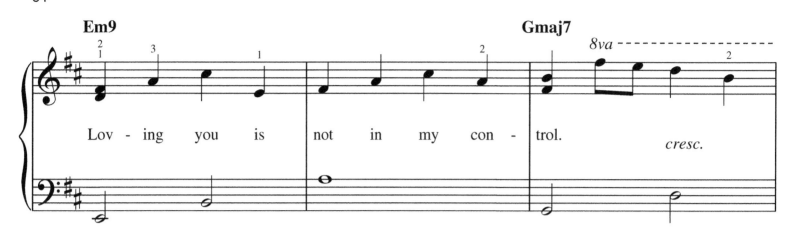

Lov - ing you is not in my con - trol.

cresc.

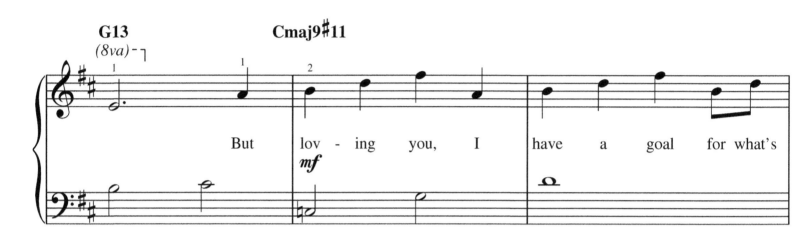

But lov - ing you, I have a goal for what's

mf

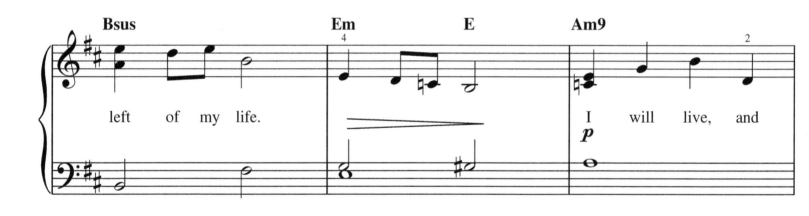

left of my life. I will live, and

p

I would die for you.

rit.

NOT WHILE I'M AROUND
from SWEENEY TODD

Words and Music by
STEPHEN SONDHEIM

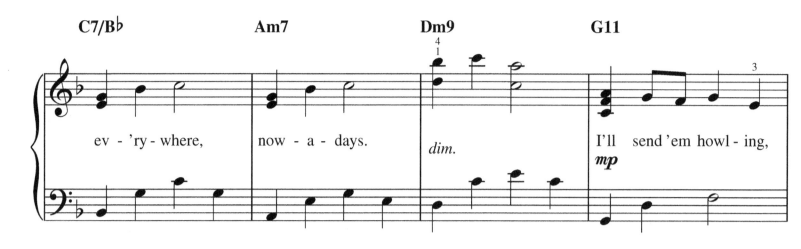

ev - 'ry - where,　now - a - days.　*dim.*　I'll　send 'em howl - ing,
mp

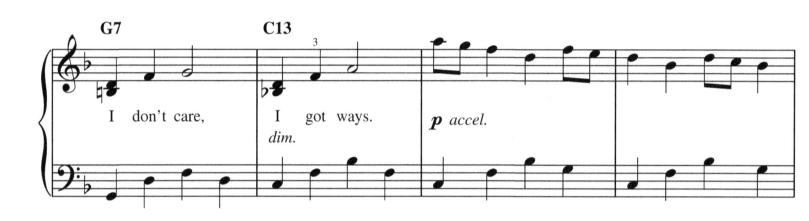

I　don't care,　I　got ways.　*p accel.*
dim.

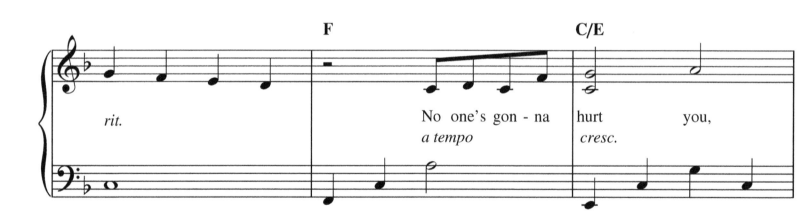

rit.　No　one's gon - na　hurt　you,
a tempo　*cresc.*

no　one's gon - na　dare.　*dim.*　*p*　Oth - ers can de -
mf

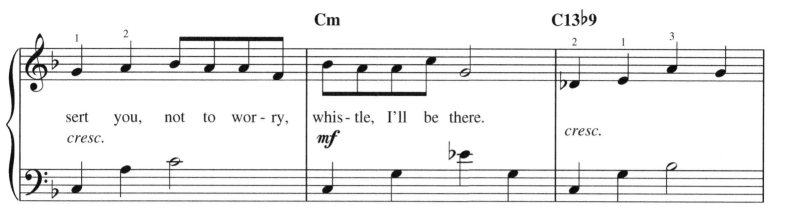

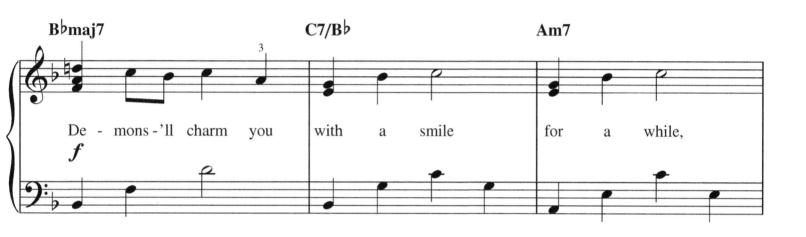

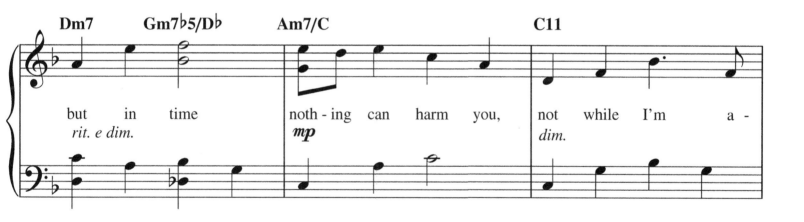

NOT A DAY GOES BY

from MERRILY WE ROLL ALONG

Words and Music by
STEPHEN SONDHEIM

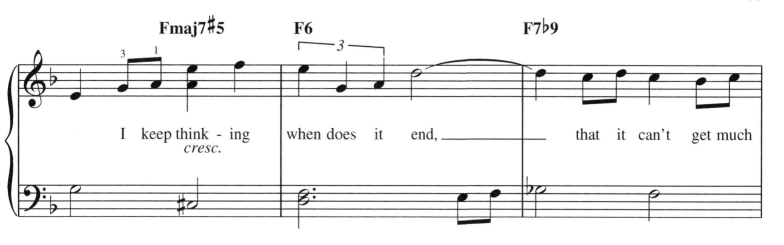

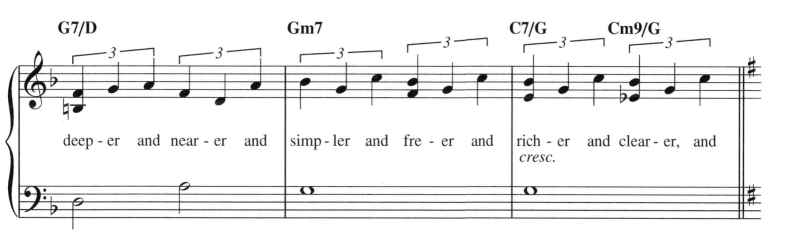

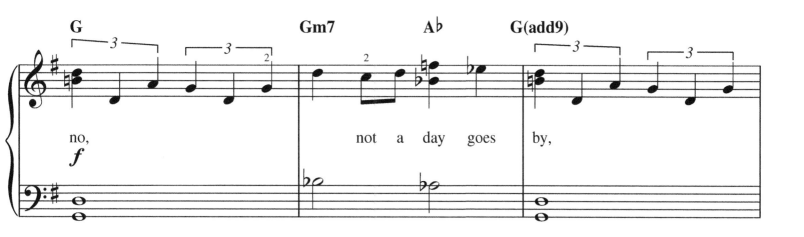

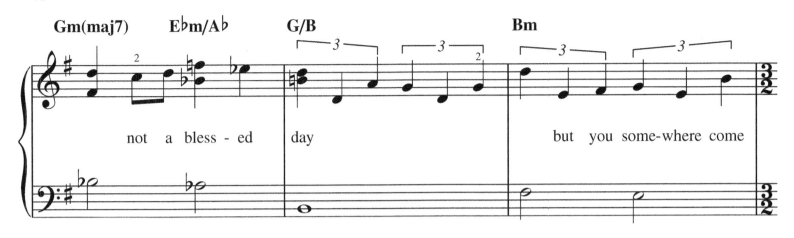

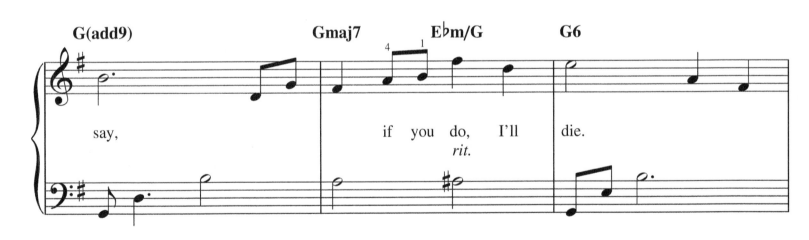

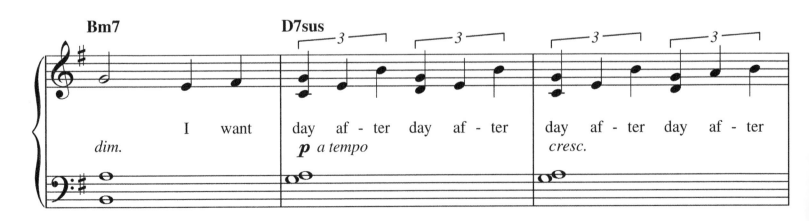

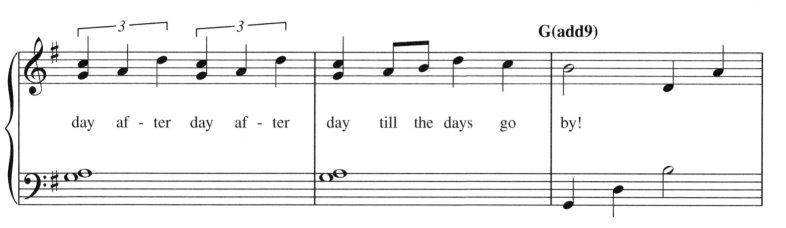

day af - ter day af - ter day till the days go by!

Till the days go by! Till the days go

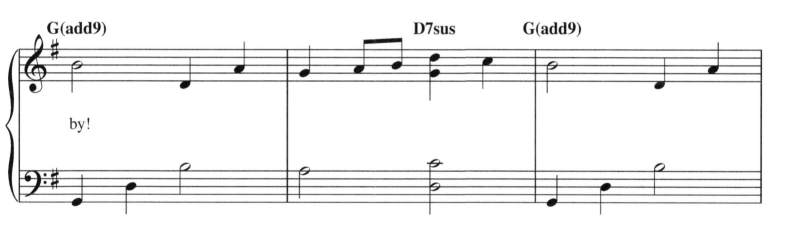

by!

Till the days go by!

OLD FRIENDS
from MERRILY WE ROLL ALONG

Music and Lyrics by
STEPHEN SONDHEIM

Hey, old

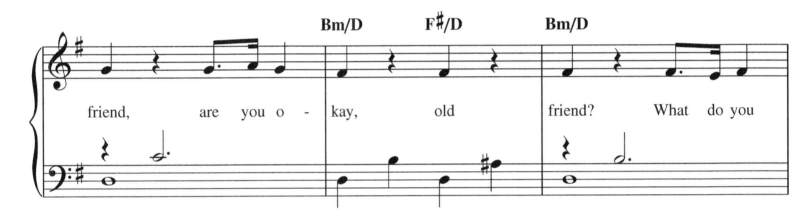

friend, are you o - kay, old friend? What do you

say, old friend, are we or are we u -

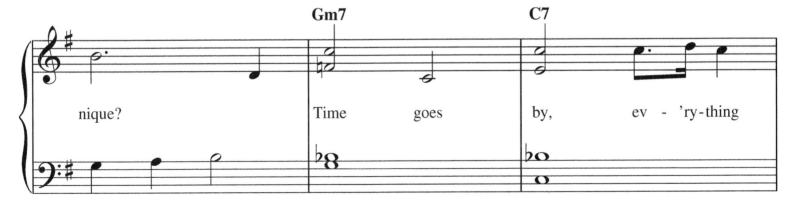

nique? Time goes by, ev - 'ry-thing

43

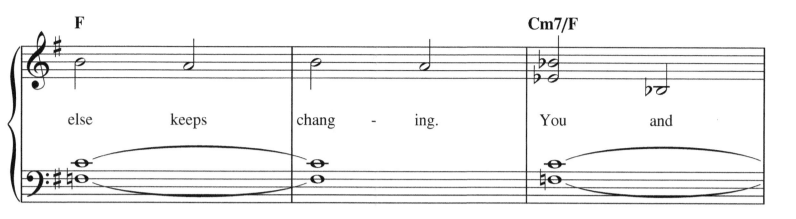

else keeps chang - ing. You and

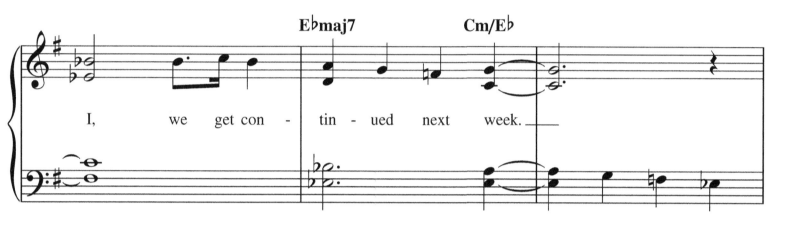

I, we get con - tin - ued next week.

Most friends fade or they don't make the

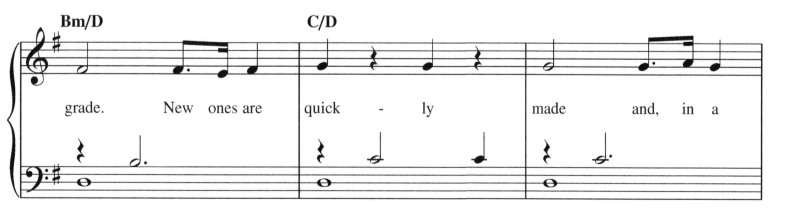

grade. New ones are quick - ly made and, in a

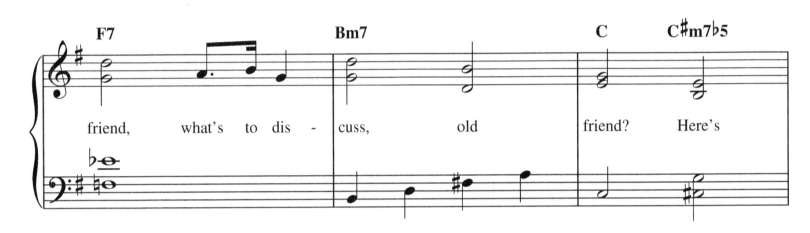

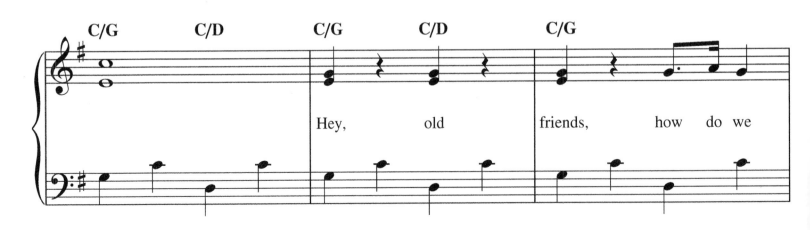

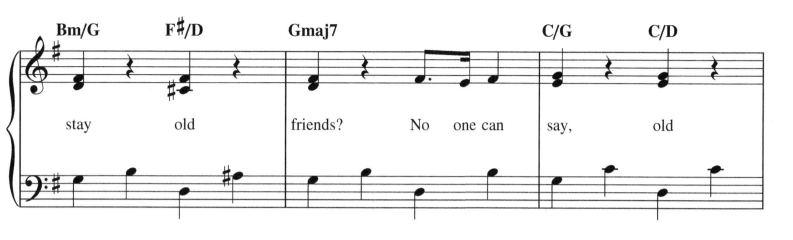

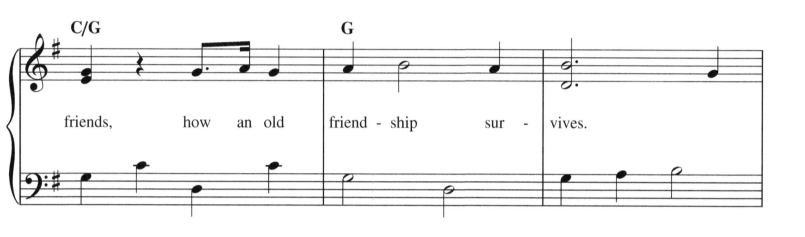

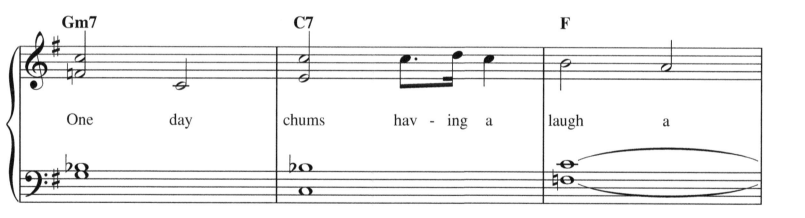

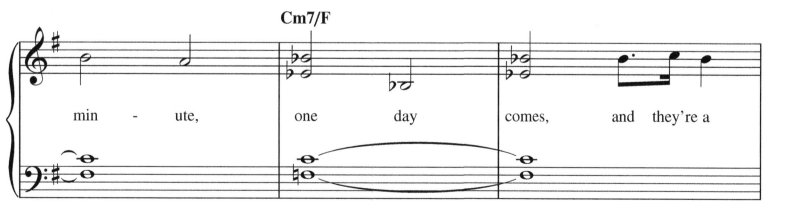

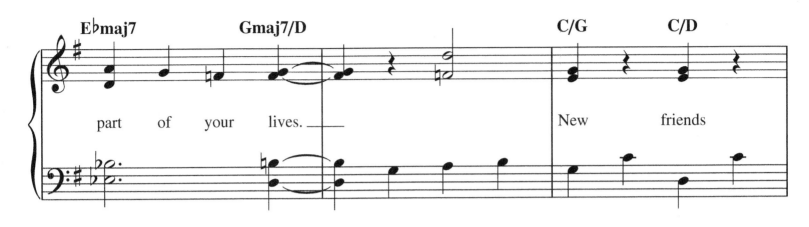

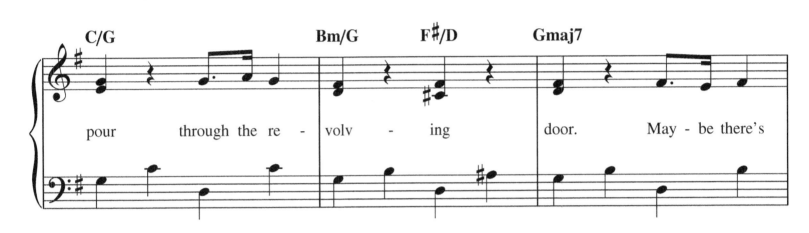

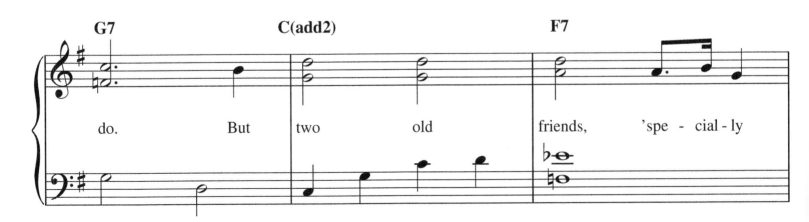

you, old friends, here's to us! Who's like us?

Two old friends, few - er won't do, old

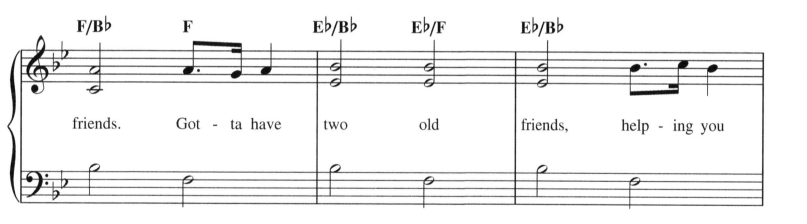

friends. Got - ta have two old friends, help - ing you

bal - ance a - long. One up -

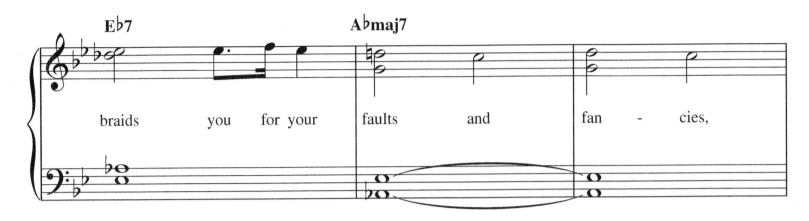

braids you for your | faults and | fan - cies,

one per - | suades you that the | oth - er one's wrong. ___

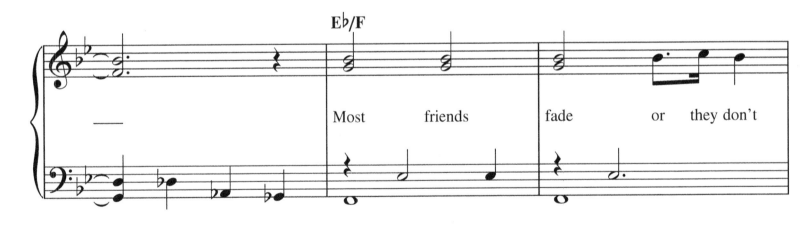

___ | Most friends | fade or they don't

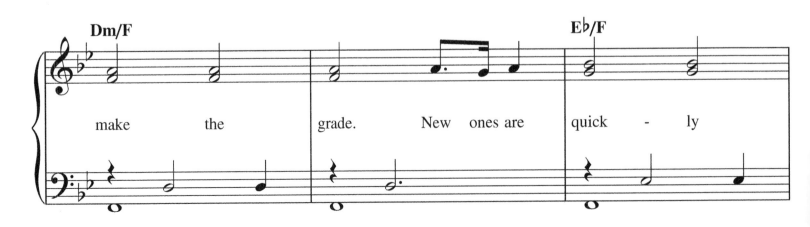

make the | grade. New ones are | quick - ly

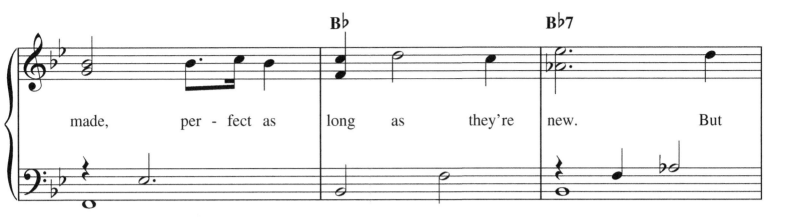

made,   per - fect as   long   as   they're   new.   But

us,   old   friends   what's   to   dis - cuss,   old

Molto rubato

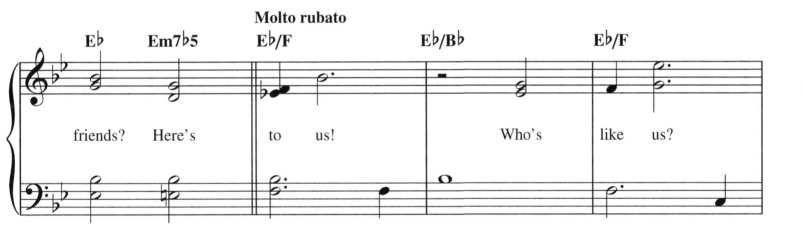

friends?   Here's   to   us!   Who's   like   us?

Damn   few! _____

PRETTY WOMEN
from SWEENEY TODD

Words and Music by
STEPHEN SONDHEIM

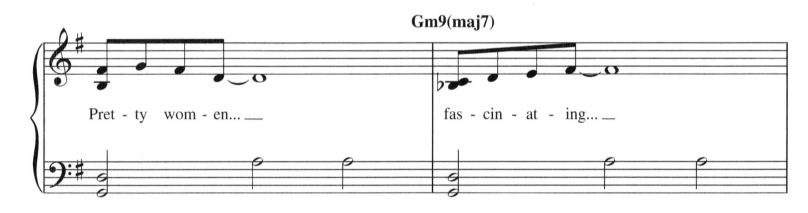

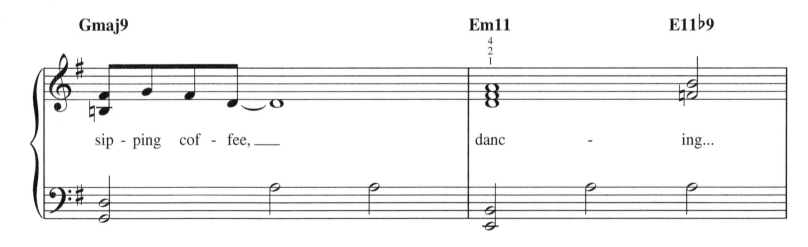

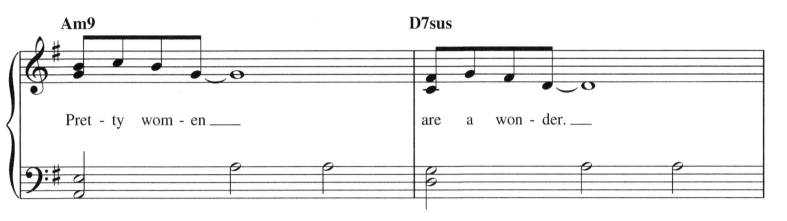

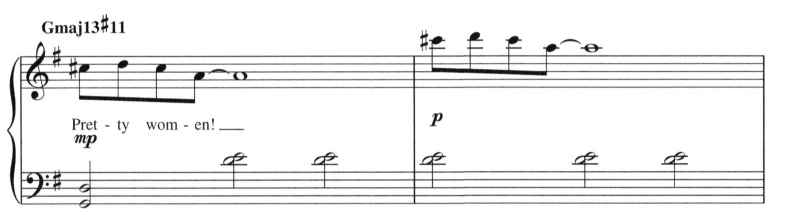

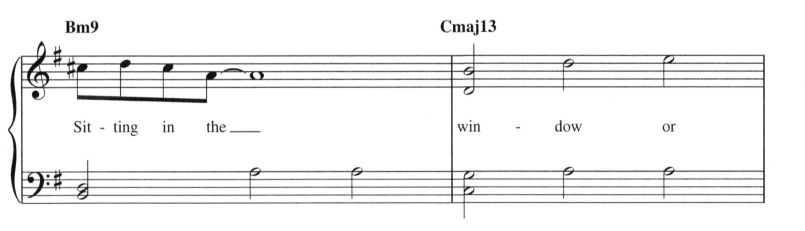

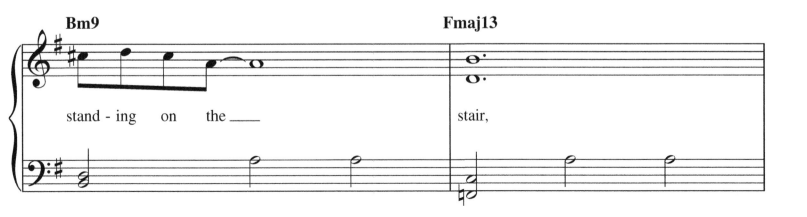

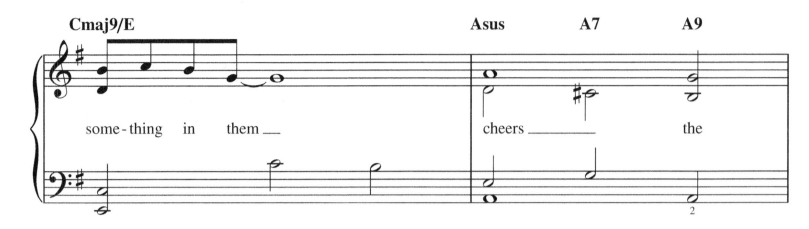

some-thing in them ____ cheers _____ the

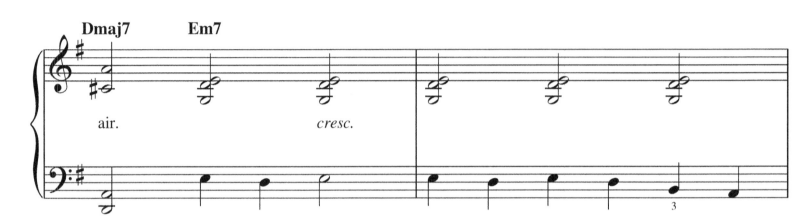

air. cresc.

Pret - ty wom - en, at their mir - rors, in their gar - den,

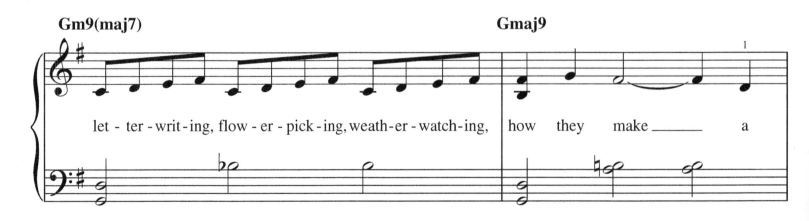

let - ter - writ-ing, flow - er - pick -ing, weath-er - watch-ing, how they make _____ a

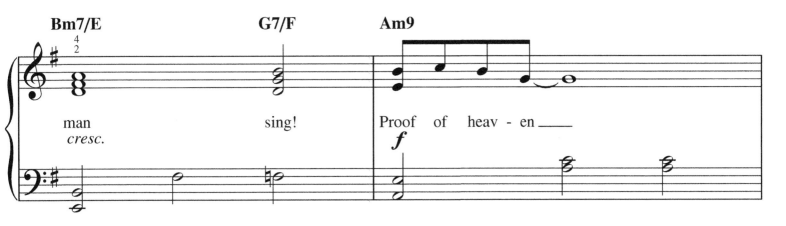

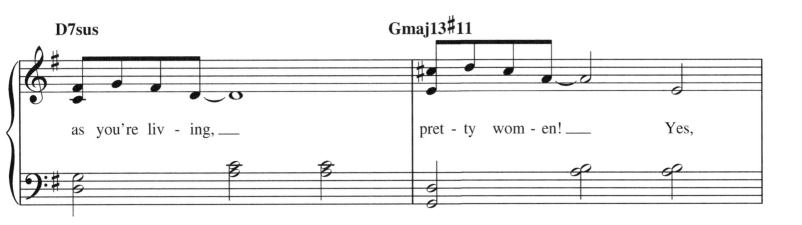

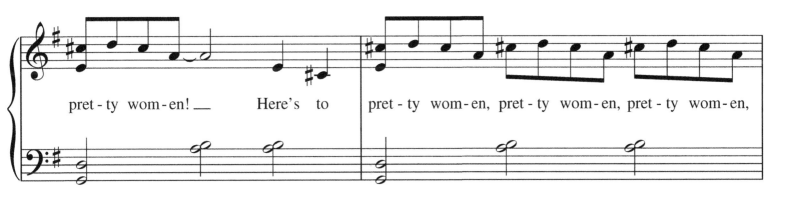

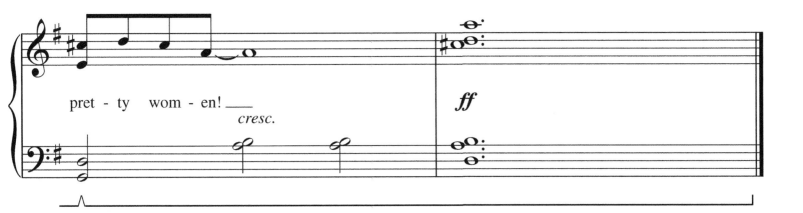

SEND IN THE CLOWNS

from the Musical A LITTLE NIGHT MUSIC

Words and Music by
STEPHEN SONDHEIM

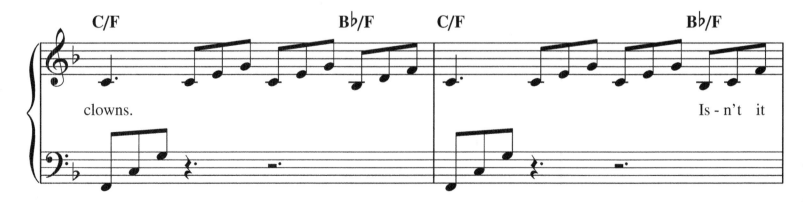

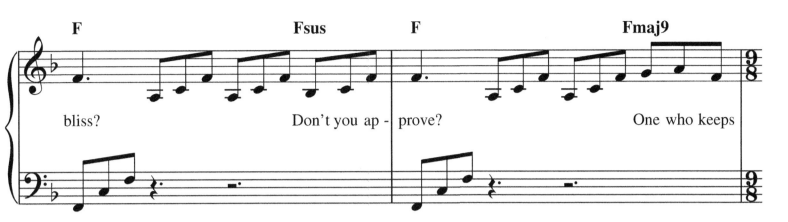

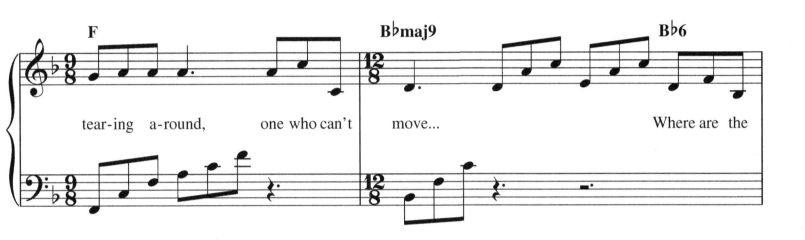

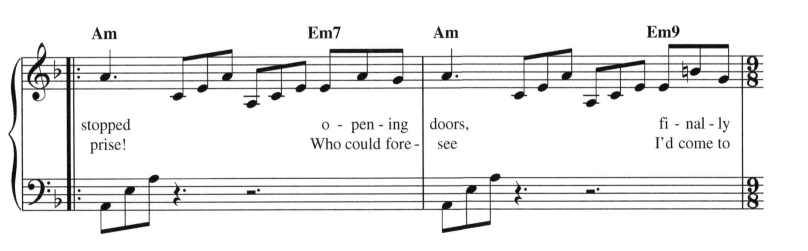

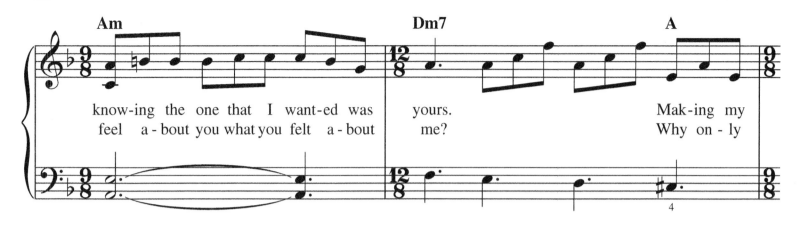

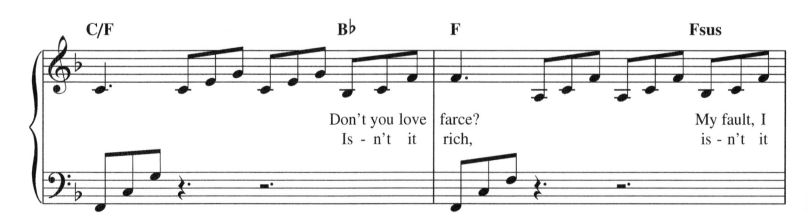

fear.
queer,
I thought that
los - ing my
you'd want what I want.
tim - ing this late
Sor - ry, my
in my ca -

dear.
reer?
But where are the
And where are the
clowns?
clowns?
There ought to   be
Quick, send in the

clowns.
Quick, send in the
clowns.
What a sur -

clowns.
Don't both-er, they're
here.

SIDE BY SIDE BY SIDE

from COMPANY

Music and Lyrics by
STEPHEN SONDHEIM

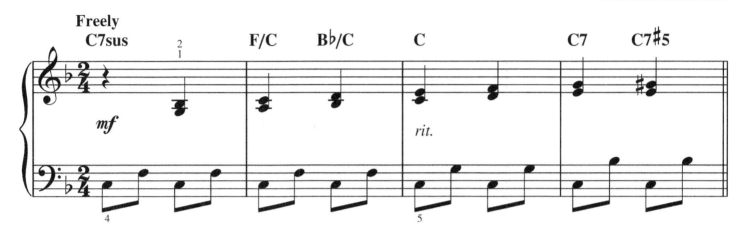

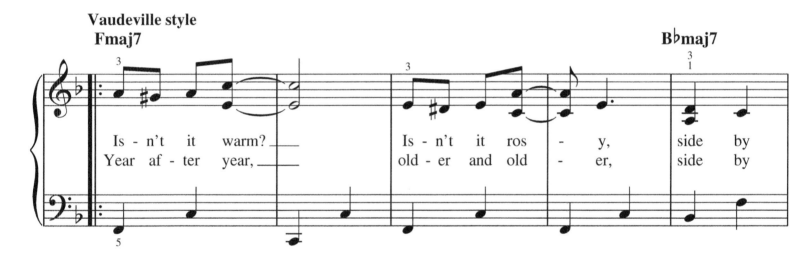

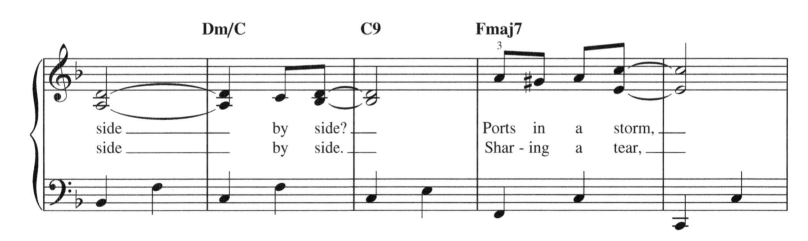

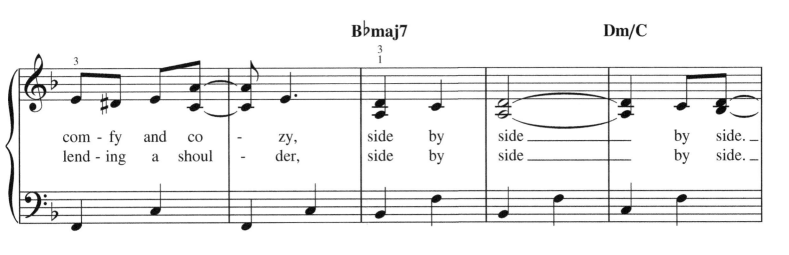

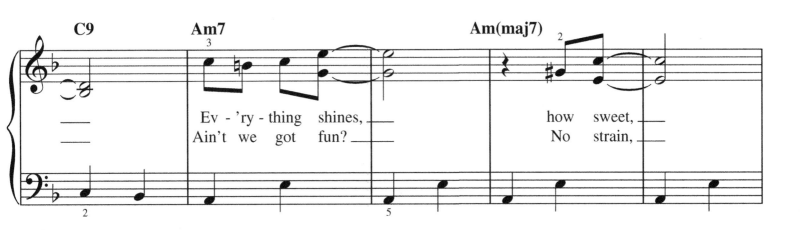

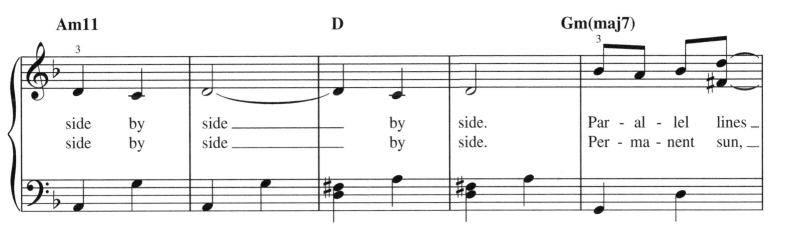

60

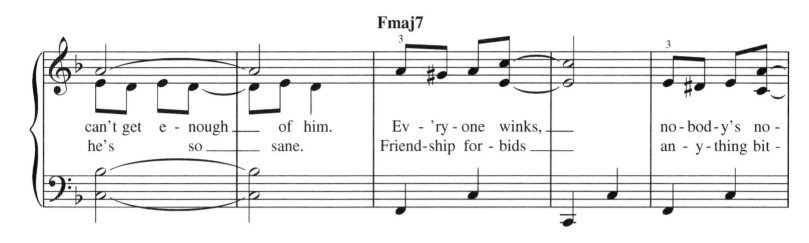

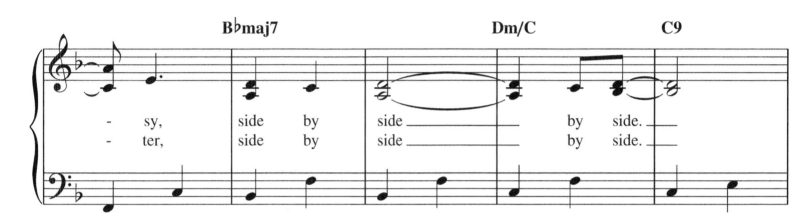

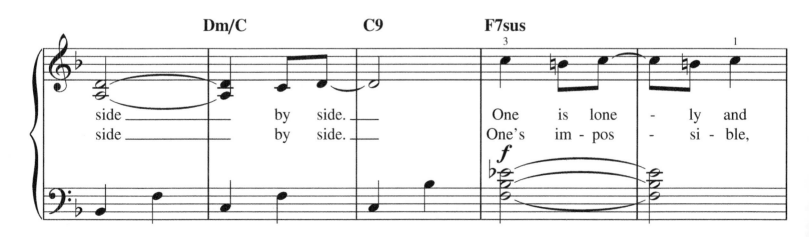

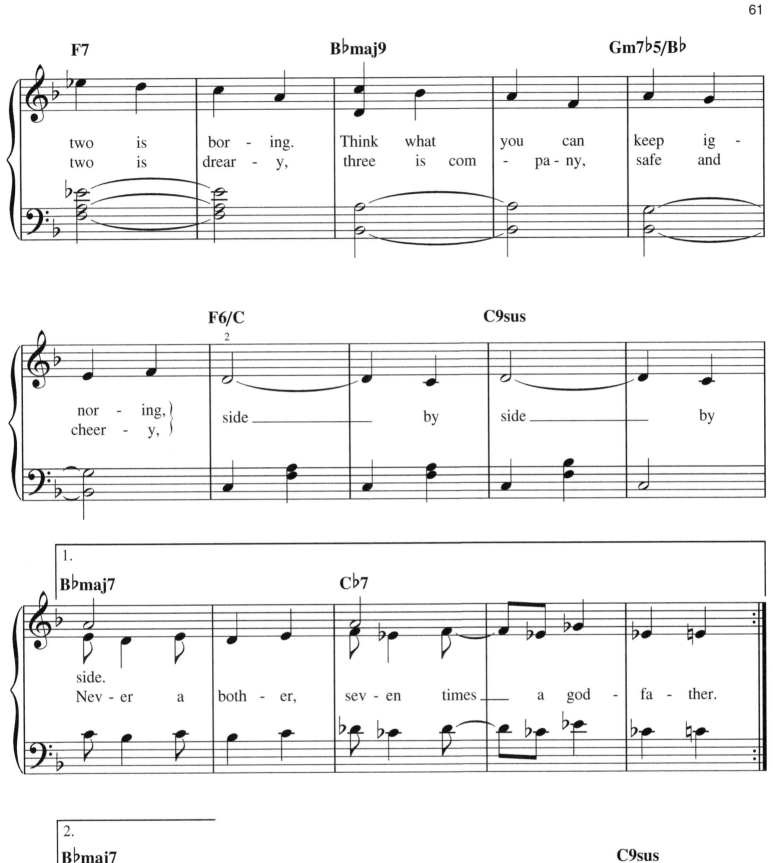

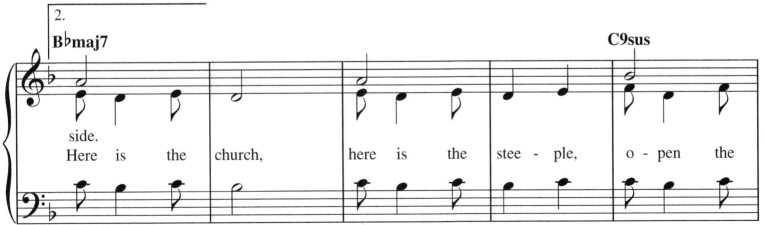

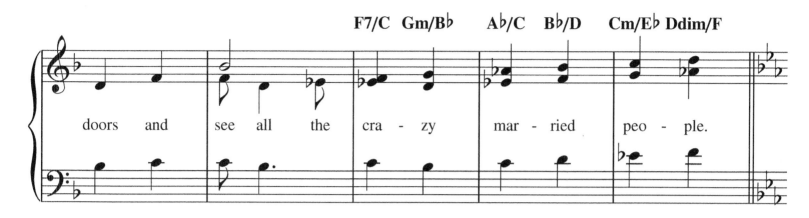

F7/C Gm/B♭ A♭/C B♭/D Cm/E♭ Ddim/F

doors and see all the cra - zy mar - ried peo - ple.

Presto

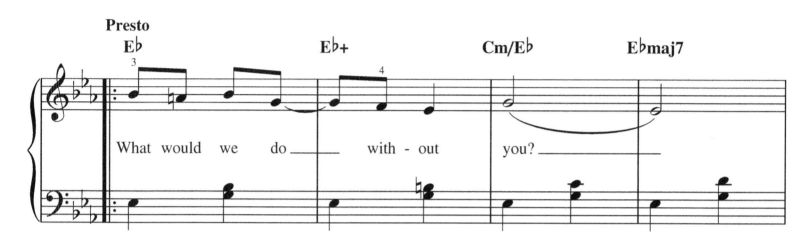

E♭   E♭+   Cm/E♭   E♭maj7

What would we do ____ with - out you? ____

Cm/E♭   E♭   F7sus   F

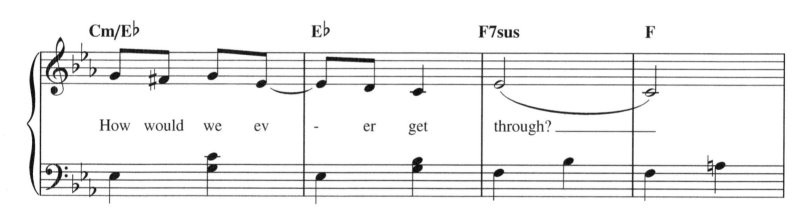

How would we ev - er get through? ____

B♭7/F   G/B   Cm

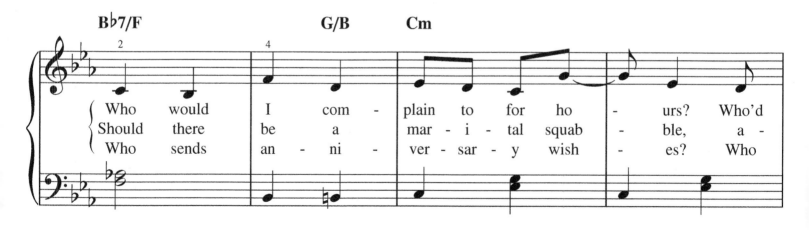

Who would I com - plain to for ho - urs? Who'd
Should there be a mar - i - tal squab - ble, a -
Who sends an - ni - ver - sar - y wish - es? Who

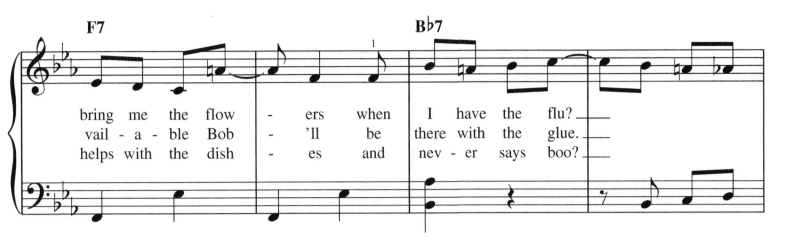

F7 ⋯ **B♭7**

bring me the flow - ers when I have the flu? ___
vail - a - ble Bob - 'll be there with the glue. ___
helps with the dish - es and nev - er says boo? ___

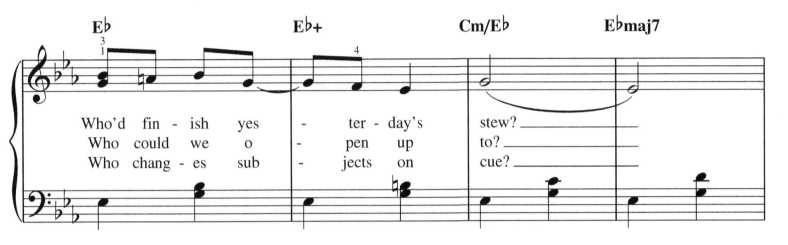

E♭ ⋯ **E♭+** ⋯ **Cm/E♭** ⋯ **E♭maj7**

Who'd fin - ish yes - ter - day's stew? ___
Who could we o - pen up to? ___
Who chang - es sub - jects on cue? ___

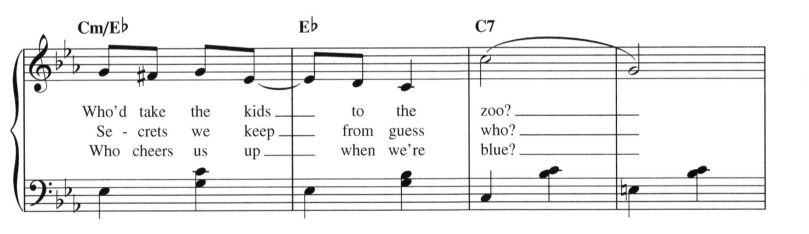

Cm/E♭ ⋯ **E♭** ⋯ **C7**

Who'd take the kids ___ to the zoo? ___
Se - crets we keep ___ from guess who? ___
Who cheers us up ___ when we're blue? ___

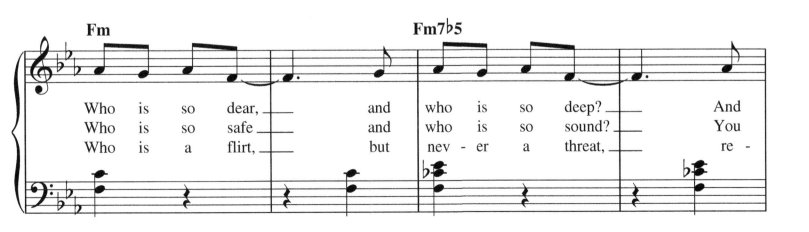

Fm ⋯ **Fm7♭5**

Who is so dear, ___ and who is so deep? ___ And
Who is so safe ___ and who is so sound? ___ You
Who is a flirt, ___ but nev - er a threat, ___ re -

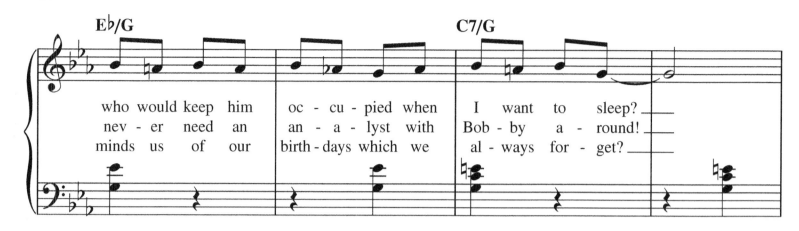

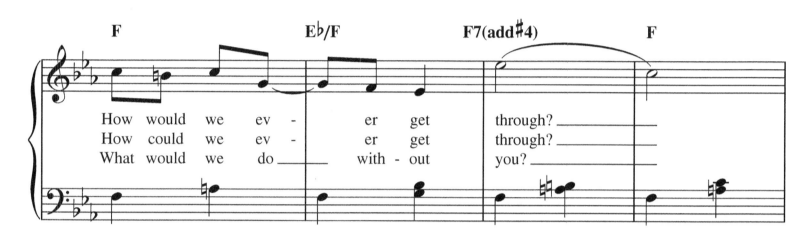

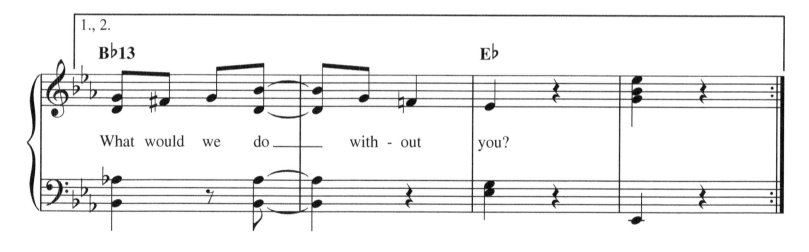

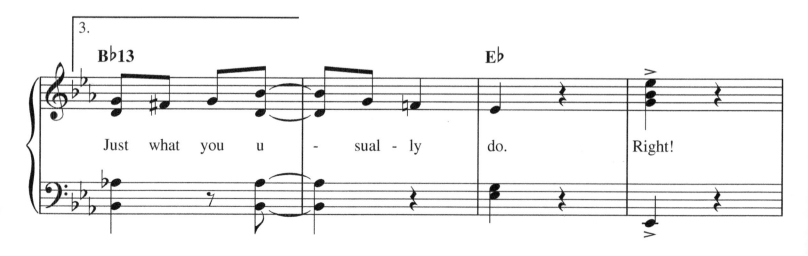

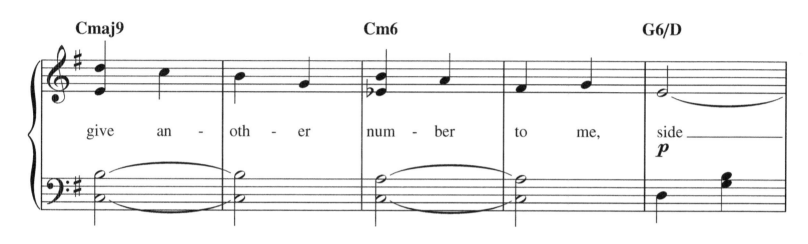

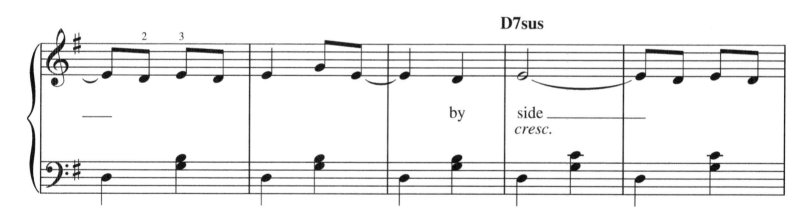

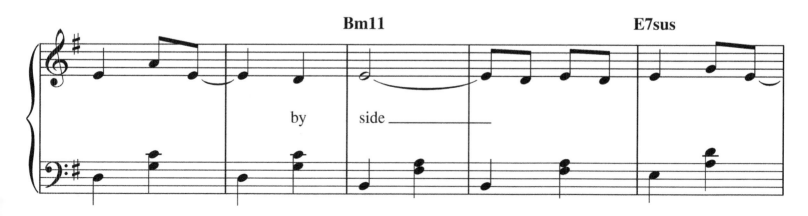

67

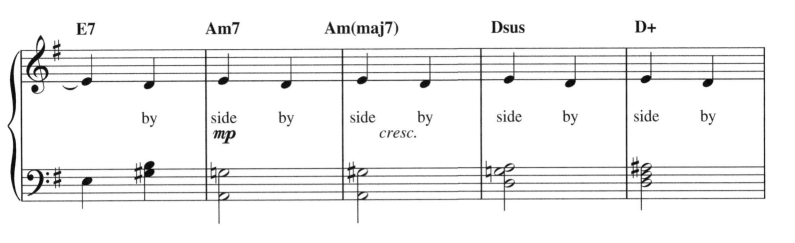

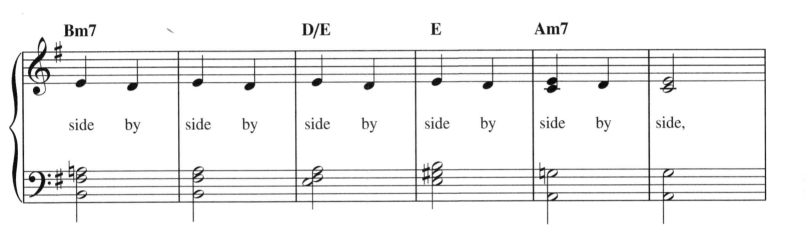

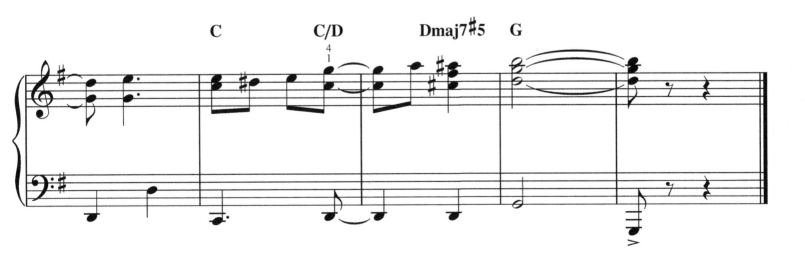

SUNDAY
from SUNDAY IN THE PARK WITH GEORGE

Words and Music by
STEPHEN SONDHEIM

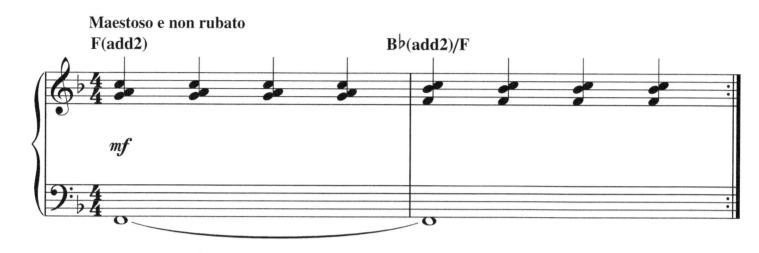

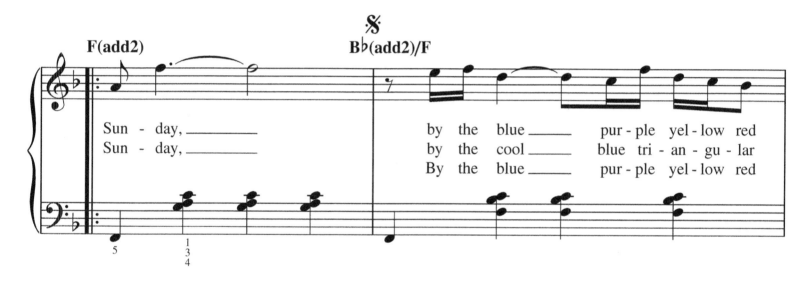

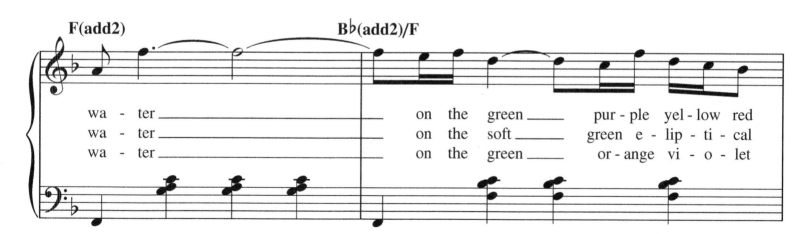

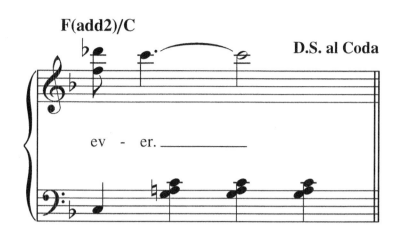

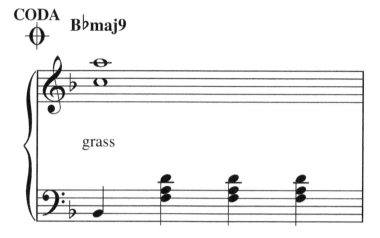

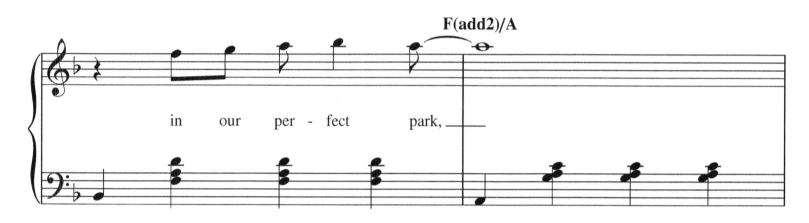

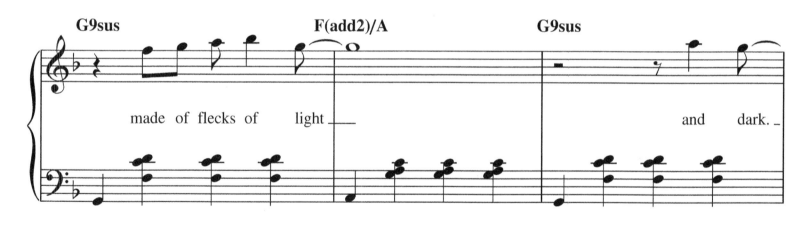

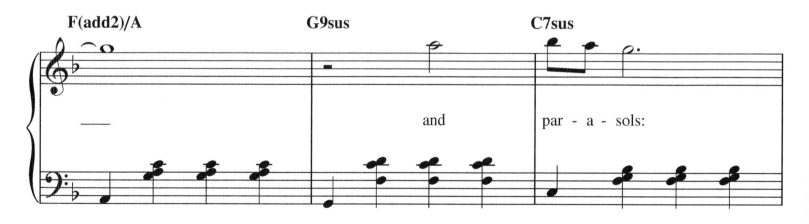

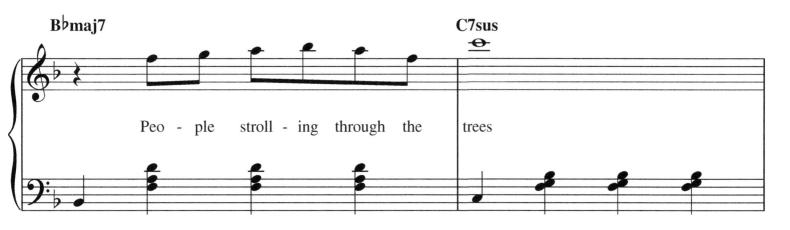

Peo - ple stroll - ing through the trees

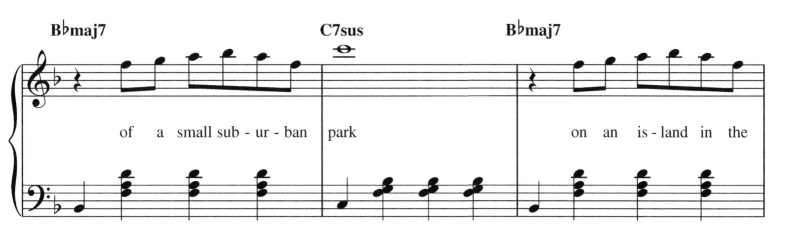

of a small sub - ur - ban park on an is - land in the

riv - er *rit.*

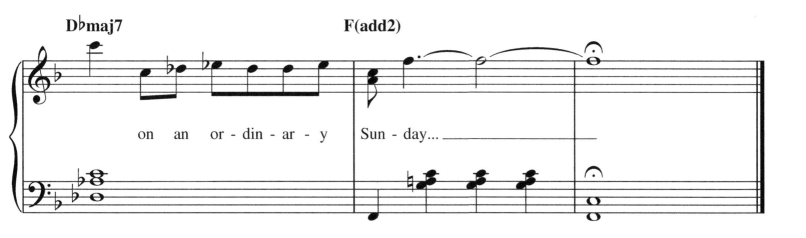

on an or - din - ar - y Sun - day... ___

STEPHEN SONDHEIM wrote the music and lyrics for *Road Show* (2008), *Passion* (1994), *Assassins* (1991), *Into the Woods* (1987), *Sunday in the Park with George* (1984), *Merrily We Roll Along* (1981), *Sweeney Todd* (1979), *Pacific Overtures* (1976), *The Frogs* (1974), *A Little Night Music* (1973), *Follies* (1971, revised in London, 1987), *Company* (1970), *Anyone Can Whistle* (1964), and *A Funny Thing Happened on the Way to the Forum* (1962), as well as lyrics for *West Side Story* (1957), *Gypsy* (1959), *Do I Hear A Waltz?* (1965), and additional lyrics for *Candide* (1973). *Side by Side by Sondheim* (1976), *Marry Me A Little* (1981), *You're Gonna Love Tomorrow* (1983), and *Putting It Together* (1992) are anthologies of his work as a composer and lyricist. For films, he composed the scores of *Stavisky* (1974) and *Reds* (1981) and songs for *Dick Tracy* (1990), for which he won an Academy Award. He also wrote songs for the television production "Evening Primrose" (1966), co-authored the film *The Last of Sheila* (1973) and the play *Getting Away With Murder* (1996), and provided incidental music for the plays *The Girls of Summer* (1956), *Invitation to a March* (1961), and *Twigs* (1971).

He won Tony Awards for Best Score for a Musical for *Passion*, *Into the Woods*, *Sweeney Todd*, *A Little Night Music*, *Follies*, and *Company*. All of these shows won the New York Drama Critics Circle Award, as did *Pacific Overtures* and *Sunday in the Park with George*, the latter also receiving the Pulitzer Prize for Drama (1985). He received a special 2008 Tony Award for Lifetime Achievement in the Theatre.

Mr. Sondheim was born in 1930 and raised in New York City. He graduated from Williams College, winning the Hutchinson Prize for Music Composition, after which he studied theory and composition with Milton Babbitt. He is on the Council of the Dramatists Guild, the national association of playwrights, composers, and lyricists, having served as its president from 1973 to 1981, and in 1983 was elected to the American Academy of Arts and Letters. In 1990 he was appointed the first Visiting Professor of Contemporary Theatre at Oxford University and in 1993 was a recipient of the Kennedy Center Honors.